Henry Thomas Smart

Thomas Cook's Early Ministry

With incidents and suggestions concerning Christian work

Henry Thomas Smart

Thomas Cook's Early Ministry
With incidents and suggestions concerning Christian work

ISBN/EAN: 9783744796514

Printed in Europe, USA, Canada, Australia, Japan

Cover: Foto ©Lupo / pixelio.de

More available books at **www.hansebooks.com**

ENGRAVED BY G COOK FROM A PHOTOGRAPH BY R H MACEY

I am Yours faithfully Thomas Cook

THOMAS COOK'S EARLY MINISTRY:

WITH

INCIDENTS AND SUGGESTIONS CONCERNING CHRISTIAN WORK.

By HENRY T. SMART,
WESLEYAN MINISTER.

LONDON:
CHARLES H. KELLY, 2, CASTLE STREET, CITY ROAD, E.C.;
AND 66, PATERNOSTER ROW, E.C.
1892.

PREFACE.

FROM the commencement of Mr. Cook's ministry as a Lay Evangelist, I have been familiar with his work, and taken a deep interest in it. It has been my lot to be associated with him in several missions. I have also had the privilege of occasionally receiving him into my house as a welcome guest.

The result has been, that a somewhat close intimacy has sprung up between Mr. Cook and myself; and during recent years we have been in the habit of conversing together in private about the subjects in which we are both profoundly interested, and which are treated upon in the following pages.

The idea of my writing an account of Mr. Cook's early ministry did not first occur to me; but when it was suggested, I was, for several reasons, not unwilling to entertain it. I knew myself to be in the fullest accord with the spirit, aims, and views of the Evangelist. I had the deepest sense of the importance of the blessed work which God has permitted him to do during the last ten years. And I was disposed to think that, if such a narrative were written, it might, by the Divine blessing, encourage God's people, and stimulate evangelists and lay preachers, and perhaps even the rising ministry of Methodism,—if I may say all that is in my heart,— to emulate the Evangelist's singleness of purpose and devotion to the Lord Jesus Christ. Now that the task is done, I can only hope that he who reads may share the blessing which has come to him who writes, as the result of this fellowship with Mr. Cook.

I wish to add, that in many instances I have given the names of the authorities for the statements I have made about the various missions. In other cases I have obtained the information either from Mr. Cook, or from his correspondence, or from friends who were connected with the work they describe. I have sometimes been able to write of Mr. Cook's missions from personal knowledge.

Care has been taken to insure perfect accuracy; and I venture to hope that it will be found by the candid reader, that the use of inflated language has been avoided; and that, however imperfect the style of the book may be when considered from the point of view of the literary man, the language is not unworthy of the writer's purpose, which is to narrate a real work of God.

The opinions expressed in the book are my own. They are the result of twenty-one years' experience in the Wesleyan-Methodist ministry, and of much meditation, not of yesterday. They are also fully shared by Mr. Cook; and therefore, whatever may be their worth, they may be accepted as the deliberate views of a Circuit minister and a Connexional Evangelist. For all personal references to Mr. Cook, I am alone responsible. It has been no part of my intention to increase his fame. I have simply wished to make it appear that an Evangelist is amongst us whose labours it has pleased God to bless in a remarkable manner.

I may add that the work is innocent of all literary pretence. It has been written during an active ministry in a London Circuit, amid many distractions; and it must therefore be judged accordingly

May the blessing of our gracious God rest upon this imperfect attempt to describe, for His glory, the special work which He has enabled His servant to do!

HENRY T. SMART.

TOTTENHAM, MIDDLESEX.

CONTENTS.

CHAP.		PAGE
I.	INTRODUCTION	1
II.	EARLY DAYS AND CONVERSION	7
III.	PREPARATION FOR WORK	20
IV.	A LAY EVANGELIST	43
V.	CONNEXIONAL EVANGELIST	69
VI.	PRINCIPLES AND METHODS OF WORK	106
VII.	HOLINESS-MEETINGS	132
VIII.	MEN'S MEETINGS	159
IX.	SEALS OF APOSTLESHIP	172
X.	CORNISH REVIVALS	194
XI.	FRAGMENTS THAT REMAIN	220
XII.	RESULTS OF THE WORK	234

THOMAS COOK'S EARLY MINISTRY

CHAPTER I.

INTRODUCTION.

THE *Lives of the Early Methodist Preachers* have been widely read, and very useful in stimulating the faith and zeal of successive generations. Those biographies show how God raised up men from amongst the multitude, and sent them to preach to the masses of the people, and how He confirmed the Word by signs and wonders. But Methodism cannot live upon the achievements of the past, how great soever those achievements may have been. God has buried all the workmen who, thanks to the diligence of the late Thomas Jackson, have been immortalised in those volumes; and buried their successors also. The great Methodist evangelists of whom we heard in our youth with amazement—Stoner, Carvosso, Bramwell, Smith—are undoubtedly dead. So are the illustrious scythesmen of a later generation. Robert Young, Peter M'Owen, Rattenbury, Vasey, Romilly Hall, Nightingale, and M'Aulay, whose bows, like the bow of Jonathan, never returned empty, are all gone hence. Is God carrying on His work?

The career of Thomas Cook is good proof that God *is* carrying on His work, and for that reason it is worthy of being published to the world. I do not hesitate to say that if competent and candid persons will examine the evidence which they will find herein, they will be convinced that no Methodist preacher of Mr. Wesley's time, or of any subsequent period, has had a more remarkable course than Thomas Cook; indeed, it may be said without exaggeration, that when all the circumstances of his ministry are considered, his work has been unique even in the romantic history of Methodism. So far as congregations are concerned, it may be said with truth that few Methodist preachers have attracted larger crowds. Within recent years popular ministers have gathered immense audiences in Methodist chapels; but the appearances of these gifted men have been rare, and the people have only had an occasional opportunity of hearing them. But in the case of Mr. Cook it has been otherwise. Night after night during two, and sometimes nearly three weeks, the largest chapels in the Connexion have proved too small to accommodate the numbers of hearers who have sought admission in order to hear Mr. Cook's message. Occasionally he has been obliged to hold two services in the same chapel on one evening, that disappointed hearers might have the opportunity, after waiting in the chapel-yard for more than an hour, until the first service was closed, of listening to the Word of Life. Whatever the multitudes went out into the wilderness to see, and whatever they may have seen, there can be no question that during the last ten years the multitudes *have* gone out " to see " Mr. Cook, and I am of opinion that it may be instructive to know what it was that the multitudes saw and heard.

If regard be had to the results of Mr. Cook's ministry, I believe it will be seen that no ministry in the history of Methodism has been more signally blessed of God. Certainly few Methodist preachers have been permitted to beget more souls in Christ Jesus through the gospel in ten years than Thomas Cook.

Possibly, however, this may be doubted by some excellent people. When Mr. Wesley laid the foundation-stone of City Road Chapel in 1777, he preached a sermon from the text, "What hath God wrought?" In the second paragraph of that sermon Mr. Wesley told his hearers that the then Bishop of London, in one of his charges, had flatly denied that God had wrought any special work in England during that century. During fifty years Mr. Wesley and his fellow-labourers had been going through the three kingdoms preaching repentance toward God and faith toward the Lord Jesus Christ, with the result that many thousands had been turned "to the wisdom of the just;" yet it seemed that the Bishop of London, who from the office he held might have been supposed to be interested in such a movement, had either not heard of what we now call "the Evangelical Revival," or, if he had heard of it, had refused to give credence to it. But the tablet in Westminster Abbey, and especially the Methodist Churches, with their twenty-five millions of adherents, abundantly prove that as "God wrought special miracles by the hands of Paul," so He wrought a special work in the British Isles in the eighteenth century by means of John Wesley.

There is not the least intention of instituting a comparison between the apostolic labours of Wesley and the brief work of Thomas Cook; all that is meant is, that if good people—aye, and even if ministers of religion—make light of the results of Mr. Cook's evangelistic labours, it will still be true that it has seemed good in the sight of God that he should be largely used to promote the edification of the body of Christ and the conversion of sinners.

The way in which Mr. Cook has been led, the work he has already done, although he is only a little more than thirty years of age, the extraordinary blessing that has rested upon his ministry, all this, it should seem, is worthy of patient and devout attention.

When Thomas Cook was thrust out by the Lord of the harvest, "he was but a youth, and ruddy, and of a fair countenance." He was of obscure parentage, without friends, without influence, without learning, endowed only with two talents, and as little likely to do "exploits for God" as David was likely to slay Goliath when he approached him with his sling and stones. For a time the Wesleyan Methodist Conference declined to accept him as a minister on trial, and he was therefore obliged to begin his career in the capacity of a lay evangelist, and without the *status* of a minister. It should also be remembered that he had not enjoyed the advantages of a collegiate course. No university conferred upon him a degree; no higher court than a local preachers' meeting authorised him to preach; and yet, as soon as he began his work, crowds flocked to hear him, and sinners were converted under his ministry.

The writer himself was travelling in the Halifax

and Bradford district when Mr. Cook accepted the invitation of the Home Mission Sub-Committee of that district to labour there as a lay evangelist, and he remembers distinctly the great success which from the first Mr. Cook enjoyed. It mattered nothing whether he was sent to what was regarded as unfruitful ground, like St. John's Chapel, Manningham, or to fruitful ground, like the Halifax Circuit; we only heard one report, which was gloriously monotonous, and was to the effect that God was causing His servant always to triumph, and was making manifest by him the savour of His knowledge in every place. The only explanation that I can offer of this circumstance—which may be said to be unprecedented in the history of Methodism, if regard is had to the preacher's extreme youth and position—is this:—

"It pleased God, who separated " Thomas Cook " from [his] mother's womb, and called [him] by His grace, to reveal His Son in [him], that [he] might preach Christ among the Gentiles."

That appears to be an adequate explanation of all that Mr. Cook has done, and it seems to be the only possible explanation that *is* adequate. "But unto every one of us is given grace according to the measure of the gift of Christ. Wherefore He saith, when He ascended up on high, He led captivity captive, and gave gifts unto men. And He gave some apostles, and some prophets, *and some evangelists*, and some pastors and teachers, for the perfecting of the saints, for the work of the ministry, for the edifying of the Body of Christ."

Can our ascended Lord bestow upon men any gift of greater value than that which He imparts when

He gives them evangelists who, being filled with the Holy Ghost and with faith, turn many people to the Lord their God?[1] And seeing that we are surrounded by large numbers of people who are without God and without hope in the world, and that we are convinced that there is a dreadful future for those who have been brought face to face with Christ in this world, and have judged themselves unworthy of everlasting life, ought we not to pray the Lord of the harvest to send forth labourers to reap as well as to sow, that both he that soweth and he that reapeth may rejoice together?

In the earnest hope that the publication of this book will prompt those who read it to offer such a prayer, and also do something to secure an answer to the petition, the writer sends it on its mission, craving pardon for its defects, and a blessing for all who shall make its acquaintance.

---

[1] See a fine sermon in the *Wesleyan Methodist Magazine* for December, by the Rev. G. G. Findlay, B.A., on "The Measure of the Gift of Christ." Mr. Findlay says, "In these gifts [of men like Wesley], for which the Church must render continued thanks, the riches of His bounty, the depth of His wisdom, and the completeness of His sovereignty are displayed to all mankind and to the end of time."

CHAPTER II.

EARLY DAYS AND CONVERSION.

THOMAS COOK was born in Middlesbrough, Yorkshire, on the 20th of August 1859. His mother was, at the time of his birth, a member of the Wesleyan Methodist Society—or Church, as we are now permitted by the resolution of the Nottingham Conference to say; but, owing to the claims of a family of little children, she was unable to attend class. It is one of the disadvantages of our most admirable ecclesiastical system, that mothers of families whose circumstances are straitened cannot possibly qualify themselves for membership with us, because it is not within their power to attend the weekly class-meeting. The same may be said of some sections of the industrial community. Omnibus and tram-car men, for example, are unable, however willing they may be, to conform to the regulations of our Church in this respect; and therefore, unless some special indulgence is shown them, they are excluded from the Society, and that through no fault of their own. As a matter of fact, a considerable number of labouring men are unavoidably shut out of our classes; and so are many mothers, whose hearts are with us, but whose maternal duties oblige them to stop at home.

We do not propose any exceptional legislation to meet the peculiar circumstances of these individuals, but we desire to commend them to the special pastoral care of the younger ministers and leaders who may not have discovered the disabilities of those for whom we plead.

When Thomas was ten years old, his parents removed into the country; and there being no Wesleyan chapel in the locality, the family attended the services of the Church of England, he and one of his brothers joining the church choir. During this time it should seem that no definite religious impressions were made upon the mind of Thomas, who, like thousands more, offered to God attendance upon religious services as a commutation for religion itself. He was, however, preserved during these and subsequent days from gross sin, and was kept by the mercy of God not far from His kingdom. It is a mistake to suppose that none but "chief" sinners become eminently useful in the Christian Church. John the Baptist, the Apostle John, Timothy, Wesley, Adam Clarke, Samuel Coley, and many other men of God, never were "chief" sinners, except in their own estimation, and yet they were "great in the sight of the Lord;" and they turned many to righteousness. We have all heard sermons on the Prodigal Son and the Elder Brother, in which the latter was condemned much more severely than the former. It is the glory of the gospel, that he who has "lien among the pots" may become "as the wings of a dove covered with silver, and her feathers with yellow gold." But it is utterly false to say that hideous sin is essential to holiness, and that, after salvation has been received, such sin is as if it had never been. A thoughtful writer has lately said: "It is a great thing to have lived a pure youth,—to have yielded to no degrading vice; to have no foul, festering secret at the heart of life. It is a great thing when we have not consciously stooped to evil,—when all men know the worst of us that is to be known, when we can die and have every drawer rummaged, and every letter read, and all the poor secrets of our history exposed, and still remain to those who loved us what we used to be. True, most true, these things will not save us. But they will make all the way of our redeemed years different. Let the young live so that when men go back to their past, and piece the divided life together, they will find all the record clean. These words of an old minister might be a talisman for the young in hours of passion and temptation: 'It is a great thing to be able to go out of this world into the other, fearless of meeting *any* spirit there. I can say that there is *no* spirit I should blush to meet.'"

In these days, when to have been a drunkard or gambler or prize-fighter is to possess a passport to the confidence of some who have charge of mission-work, it is well to remember that the Christian Church owes more to those who entered the vineyard early in the day than to those who entered later, and that *some* who are "first" shall continue "first," and *some* who are "last" shall remain "last." There is nothing contrary to this in our Lord's words.

After three years' residence in the country, Thomas Cook returned to the Middlesbrough Circuit, and joined the congregation which worshipped in the South Bank Wesleyan Chapel. Methodist preaching soon began to impress the youth, old impressions were revived, the good Spirit worked graciously in his heart, and he was led to turn wistful eyes towards the "Lamb of God, which taketh away the sin of the world." It may here be said, that when Thomas was a child of seven years of age he heard the late Rev. James Nance preach from the text, "And I heard the voice of harpers harping with their harps," and received impressions which he never lost, and which must be included amongst the various causes which led to his early and thorough conversion. From the day he heard that sermon, eternal things were to him, to use his own language, "tremendously *real*." Nor need we be surprised at this. At five years of age Samuel Coley enjoyed a distinct consciousness of God's favour, and never did he lose the blessing. And yet most of us are indisposed to believe in the conversion of children, as though foolishness were so bound up in the heart of a child that not even the grace of God could eradicate it.

Perhaps it is owing to this unbelief that there is a tendency just now to withdraw the scholars of our Sunday schools from the services in the chapel, and to provide for them short services in the school-room, which, it is supposed, will be better adapted to their capacity. We believe this to be a mistake, excepting in the case of very young children; and even concerning them we have our doubts. Children should be trained in the habit of attending the house of God. Suitable seats —not too high—should be given them, and the expectation should be cherished that the services will benefit them as much as other worshippers. Preachers themselves will judge whether or not they should give a brief address to the children before commencing to preach; but if this is not done, care should be taken to let a few crumbs fall from the pulpit for the children at every service. The writer has seen this done with great effect by Mr. Spurgeon and Dr. Parker, to whom children often listen with almost as much pleasure as do adults.

Thomas Cook joined the Sunday school about this time, and was there brought under influences that contributed largely to promote his conversion. His Sunday-school teacher may be described as the Rev. John M'Neill described himself in an appeal which he circulated a while ago in the London workshops, namely, as "a railway man." He was, as a matter of fact, a porter at a railway station, with no better education than men of his class usually have; but he was a tender, patient, loving, Christ-like man, and withal a man of good sense, whose consistent and winsome life perhaps did more to bring the future Evangelist to Christ than all the sermons he heard in those days. Not that the preaching of the Word of God is to be disparaged. We have already seen that a profound and permanent impression was made upon the mind of Thomas Cook when he was but a child by the preaching of the Word, and we desire to magnify the preacher's office. There is an absurd disposition manifested now-a-days, —and that sometimes in quarters from which better things might be looked for,—to speak lightly of sermons, as though they were as much out of date as spinning-wheels. When preachers raise or join in this outcry against preaching, it may be supposed that they are led to do so by reflecting upon the quality and effects of their own sermons, and that they are measuring other ministers' corn with their own bushel. Whether the preaching of the gospel be appreciated or not, it is true to say that, until the sign of the Son of man appears in heaven, it will please God "by the foolishness of preaching" to save them that believe. These words are a quotation from the New Testament; but when they are cited for the purpose of discrediting God's appointed means for bringing men to a knowledge of the truth, they are misapplied. St. Paul never intended to suggest that preaching is a foolish employment; what he meant to say was, that the subject-matter of evangelical preaching appears to men to be foolishness. These observations seem necessary, lest it should be supposed that we wish to detract from the honour which belongs to the preached Word when we affirm that the railway porter's beautiful Christian life more deeply impressed Thomas Cook than did the sermons which he heard. All honour to this Sunday-school teacher, and to the order of Christian workers which he represents. It is not known that this labouring man was the means of the conversion of any one beside Mr. Cook; nor is it true to say that he was the sole cause of his conversion, since Thomas Cook was the child of many prayers. But this railway porter had more to do with effecting the immediate decision of the youth than any one else excepting his praying mother.

"There was a little city, and few men within it; and there came a great king against it, and besieged it, and built great bulwarks against it. Now there was found in it a poor wise man, and he, by his wisdom, delivered the city; yet no man remembered that same poor man." The Sunday-school teacher is "that same poor man;" for, by his "wisdom," he has delivered this kingdom from many evils. Not many years ago there came to this country a distinguished publicist to investigate the condition of the people, and the way in which they are affected by our laws, especially by our land laws. When he had fulfilled his mission he put on record his impressions of England. He expressed dissatisfaction with some of our laws, and proceeded to ask how it was that, notwithstanding what appeared to him to be oppressive customs, the English people were law-abiding and prosperous. He found the answer to his question in the practical character of our religion, and especially in the circumstance that that religion is inculcated in the minds of some millions of young people every Sunday by more than six hundred thousand Sunday-school teachers. This witness is true. Yet who remembers this "same poor man"? Not the British Government, which rewards with a coronet the successful brewer, and ignores the services of all Sunday-school teachers. Nor does the typical Mayor remember this "poor man;" for while many Mayors are willing to do honour to fillibusters whose proceedings abroad have sullied the honour of the English nation, few are ready publicly to recognise the disinterested labours of Sunday-school teachers who are endeavouring to train up the children that come streaming into England, in the faith and fear of God, and to make them Christian men and women. But it is written, "And they that be teachers (margin) shall shine as the brightness of the firmament; and they that turn many to righteousness as the stars for ever and ever," Dan. xii. 3.

In 1875, Mr. Cook, being then sixteen years old, was "powerfully" converted, as our American friends term it. The circumstances were as follows.

The local preachers of the Middlesbrough Circuit were holding a series of special services. Thomas Cook had long been waiting for an opportunity publicly to avow himself as a disciple of Christ, and he resolved that he would embrace the opportunity which this mission afforded for carrying out his purpose. He had not that deep sense of personal sinfulness which many penitents have, who cry to God out of the depths to make the bones which He has broken to rejoice. This, however, need excite no surprise, for prevenient grace had kept him from presumptuous sins, and he was innocent of the great transgression. But he had a profound sense of the paramount claims of the Lord Jesus Christ, and the crisis through which he passed took the form of a deliberate response to those claims, as in the case of him who said, "Lord, what wilt Thou have me to do?" He was under the influence of considerations, such as are advanced by the Rev. W L. Watkinson in the first chapter of his useful book, *The Beginning of the Christian Life*. That chapter is entitled "Begin Early," and it is devoted to a number of cogent reasons for commencing the Christian life in the days of youth. Therein we read: "The best that a man has is himself, and his young undebauched life is himself at his best." God be praised, that Thomas Cook's life never was debauched, and that it was dedicated to God when it was "no mean sacrifice."

During the mission of which we are writing, Thomas Cook accepted the invitation that was given by the preacher to penitents, and went forward to the communion rail, and with dry eyes solemnly espoused himself to Christ. The consciousness of his acceptance with God came to him gradually rather than suddenly, which is an instructive circumstance for those who have to do with new-born souls.

During that same year a young minister, who had been used by God during his probation, and who since then has been permitted to do much blessed work for Christ, stood by the writer's side at the Sheffield Conference, and gave, as is customary, a brief account of his conversion and call to the ministry. He remarked that he was not sure of the hour when his chains fell off, and he added that he believed that his chains *were* off; but of this *one* thing he was sure —they *were* off. The name of that young minister was Edward Smith, and his experience may fittingly be recorded here because it tallied exactly with that of Mr. Cook. True, most true it is, that God does not impart the forgiveness of sins to any in a piecemeal fashion, remitting some sins to-day and others to-morrow; and equally true it is that He sometimes overwhelms the penitent with an instant and unmistakeable assurance of His favour, which causes him to exclaim,—

"O 'tis more than I can bear,
The sense of pardoning love."

But that gracious Spirit, who is as the wind which bloweth as it listeth, is pleased gradually to convince some persons of sin, and gradually to assure them that they are accepted in the Beloved. This was Mr. Cook's experience. Day by day the Lord Jesus

Christ became more real to him, and day by day his enthusiastic love for his Saviour increased.

There was no great rejoicing amongst the mission workers at South Bank that night, for only one conversion had taken place, and the solitary convert was but a lad. But "things are not what they seem." There was joy in the presence of the angels of God, however, over the repentance of one sinner; and there was joy in a mother's heart because a son had been brought to Christ, and especially because the son was the one child of the family whose conversion seemed to her most improbable. The parents of Jabez called him by that name because it signified "sorrow," and it was with special sorrow that his mother bore him. Yet he became "more honourable than his brethren," and his "ways" and his "doings" were such, that when his parents saw them, the son "comforted" his parents, as we read in the Book of Ezekiel. So it was in the case of Thomas Cook, who, like many other lads, has become a better man than his mother ever dreamed he would become.

It is worthy of remark that neither the preacher of that evening nor his sermon had anything to do with Thomas Cook's conversion. Many influences contributed to this result,—particularly the efforts of the Sunday-school teacher, — but this mission service became the occasion of his decision "for God to live and die." How many persons are there in our congregations in exactly the same condition as young Cook was in when he attended this special service! He was "not far from the kingdom of God," and yet he was not consciously and avowedly in it; and it was possible that whilst he was "almost persuaded" he might yet be lost. What he needed was, to be brought to decision; and this is what many now need, especially many young people who have been brought up in Christian homes. The Rev. Dr. Gregory has justly said, in a sermon published by him in the *Wesleyan Methodist Magazine* for October 1870, that "even children of devoted parents, though 'heaven' *did* lie 'about us in our infancy,' and though the claims of the law and the love of God pressed like a Presence on us day and night; even we cannot evade the command, 'Come out, and be separate, and I will receive you; and ye shall be My sons and daughters, saith the Lord Almighty.' *The decisive movement must be made.*" The late Benjamin Alfred Gregory, whose premature death, as we are apt to think it was, we have not ceased to lament since we read the *Memorials* of him which his accomplished father published a few years ago, intimated to Dr. Gregory that these sentences were descriptive of his own experience. That gifted youth made "the decisive movement," when, on the eve of the first Sunday in the year 1865, he went to his father's study, and with strong emotion asked leave to attend the Covenant service on the following day. That step formed the crisis of his life; henceforth he was a Christian man. Hereafter, we shall have occasion to refer to the late Rev. Dr Punshon, and we may therefore be permitted to cite his conversion, as another instance of what is meant. Morley Punshon was walking on the dockside in Hull on the 29th of November 1838, he being then in his fifteenth year, when he was met by the late Rev S. Romilly Hall, who urged upon the youth the necessity of immediate belief. "Then and there," said the orator of modern Methodism, "I was enabled to lay hold on my Saviour, and peace immediately sprang up in my heart." We thus see that it is necessary to aim at the immediate conversion of those who, although they are not far from the kingdom of God, lack "one thing." Mission services often effect this, and hence their great value. But the same end would more frequently be attained in the ordinary services of the churches than it now is, if those who conduct them were more peremptory in their appeals, and set their hearts more earnestly on immediate results. In all congregations, it may reasonably be supposed, there are young people in whom "there is some good thing toward the Lord God of Israel," but who are not yet decided Christians. Yes, "the decisive movement must be made," and Circuit ministers may reap and receive "wages," and gather "fruit unto eternal life," as well as Connexional evangelists, if they will encourage their hearers, in season and out of season, to make this "movement," and to leave all and follow Christ. Who can fortell the consequences of a single conversion? When the boy Spurgeon, at the bidding of the good Primitive Methodist local preacher, looked to the Lamb of God and was saved, no one dreamed of the exploits for God which he was destined to achieve; for, like St. Paul, he was "a chosen vessel," as also was Thomas Cook. We must learn to value the conversion of single souls. The Methodist newspapers would lightly esteem a mission service at which only one convert was made; and the story of such a service would excite but languid interest if told in the Conference during the conversation on the Work of God. And yet what immense consequences have followed a solitary conversion! Some of the seed which is the Word of God brings forth "an hundred fold" when sown on "good ground." The devoted founder of the Joyful News Mission, who is now bearing in his body the brand-marks of the Lord Jesus, went on one occasion to a small village to conduct a mission service, when he was labouring in the Bolton district as a missionary. There were only seven persons present at that service, and had the preacher offered prayer, and then "dismissed the assembly," as the town clerk of Ephesus did, who would have blamed him? Mr. Champness, however, yielded to no such temptation, but threw himself as heartily into the service as though seven thousand had been present. The result was that he begot one soul in Christ Jesus through the gospel on that occasion, and the convert thus gained has become a pillar of the little village church to which he was "added," under circumstances that would have depressed a less courageous man than our beloved brother. "Whatsoever thy hand findeth to do, do it with thy might."

When Zilpah bore Jacob a son, Leah said, "A troop [of children] cometh;" and when "this man," of whose work we write, was "born" of God "in Zion," at that apparently unimportant service, a similar exclamation might have been made by any bystander who had skill enough to cast the horoscope, for Thomas Cook's conversion has led to the conversion of troops of souls.

CHAPTER III.

PREPARATION FOR WORK.

THE genuineness of Mr. Cook's conversion was immediately proved by the zeal for the salvation of others which at once took possession of him. If any man has the Spirit of Christ, he is His, whether his conversion was effected suddenly or gradually, and accompanied by ecstatic joy or quiet peace. Thomas Cook had the Spirit of Christ, and hence he at once made earnest attempts to save others. He waited for no authorisation, for no leader to set him to work, for no new organisation to be set afoot; he set himself to work. He began his successful evangelistic labours by quietly commending his Saviour to individuals.

He resolved that he would let no day pass without speaking to at least one person about personal religion, and to this resolution he owes his first two converts and much of his later usefulness.

When crossing the road shortly after he had formed this purpose, Mr. Cook chanced to see a man pushing a hand-cart. Accosting him, the youth asked if he loved the Saviour; and thereupon the man replied, with water standing in his eyes, as Bunyan would have said, that although he was not a Christian, he wished to be one, as also did his wife. Name and address were obtained, an appointment for an interview at the close of the day was made and kept, and ere bedtime came the youth had led the man and his wife to Christ, and found, as George Herbert teaches, that

> "All earthly joys grow less
> To the one joy of doing kindliness."

It was thus that this reaper gathered his first sheaves. That night the future evangelist acquired a taste for soul-saving which has grown into what Alleine calls "an insatiable greed for souls." He soon began to speak for his Master in the open air. God be praised, the streets are always open to any earnest man who longs to turn the hearts of "the disobedient unto the wisdom of the just." It is sometimes said that many Methodists are pining for Christian work, and that unless these unemployed persons are organised and set to do something, they will leave Methodism, and go where they will be likely to find scope for their energy and ability.

The successful pastor will always aim at making his people a working church, and will be satisfied with nothing less than driving every wheel in the machinery to its utmost power. He will make it his duty to prevent any member who joins his church from settling down into a mere "passenger," and he will be anxious to do as little himself as he can, in order that he may spend his strength in arousing all the latent power of his congregation. But if it is not the privilege of all church members to be directed by pastors of this kind, why should not those who are under less capable or less faithful direction imitate our evangelist, and set themselves to work? One of the greatest pulpit geniuses of the day, Dr. Parker, told a number of Wesleyan Methodist ministers who met him in conference early in the year 1891, at Wesley's Chapel, City Road, that it was in this way that he began his splendid ministerial career. Dr. Parker was present at an open-air service on one occasion, when, feeling that he had a message for the people, he asked leave of the preacher to address the crowd. Borrowing the preacher's Bible, as well as his congregation, young Parker faced the throng, and read in their hearing the verse which with characteristic audacity he had chosen as his text, and which reads thus: "If I whet my glittering sword, and mine hand take hold on judgment; I will render vengeance to mine enemies, I will reward them that hate me." From that day Dr. Parker has never lacked opportunities to preach that gospel which during the last one-and-twenty years he has so powerfully proclaimed from the pulpit of the City Temple. Long may his light continue to shine! Let the young unemployed Christian, who aspires to the ministry, win his spurs in the streets. Let him do the duty that lies nearest to him, and then his future duty will become clear. A newly-converted engine-driver went to a brother minister of the writer's and asked for "work." The minister inquired if the engine-driver had a stoker with him on his engine. When told that such was the case, he further asked if the stoker was a converted man. The reply was "No." "Then," said the minister, "go and seek to save *him*." The advice was taken, and the happiest results followed.

> ' I would not have the restless will
>   That hurries too and fro,
> Seeking for some great thing to do,
>   Or secret thing to know:
> I would be treated as a child,
>   And guided where I go."

Young unemployed Methodists who "want a field of labour" may find it "anywhere," as Mr. Cook did. A youth intimated to Thomas Cook that he was wishful to join him in open-air work, and that he was preparing a small platform to serve as a street pulpit. The overture was accepted, and the two boys, like St. Paul and Philemon, became "partners." The platform proved to be a sort of huge green box, having handles at both ends, and the words, "Stand up for Jesus," inscribed on the front in brass letters. "This is our pulpit," said the youth, who himself had made it, and now proposed to use it. "Take hold of it; we shall soon get a congregation." Each boy seized a handle, and soon they were in the street with their load. Nor had they to wait long for hearers. The peculiar box, and perhaps the youthful appearance of the speakers, attracted a little crowd, and to them the boys told what they knew of the love of God in Christ. When Gideon Ouseley was contemplating beginning his evangelistic course, he hesitated for a while to take up the burden, on the ground that he was unprepared for the duty. But he was prompted to obey the Lord's call by what seemed to him an inward voice saying, "Gideon, you know the disease; do you not?" "Yes," was his reply; "sin is the disease." "And you know the remedy?" "Yes, God be praised, it is the gospel of Christ." "Then," said the voice, "go and tell the people of the disease and the remedy; all else is mere talk." When Thomas Cook first stood on that box he only knew the disease and the remedy, but he had such a practical knowledge of these that he was able to speak to purpose. Precious memories gathered around that green box, which Mr. Cook now preserves amongst his treasures, as David preserved the sword of Goliath, and for much the same reason.

When Thomas Cook, two years after his conversion, left South Bank, and returned with his parents to Middlesbrough, he joined the Society class of Mr. George Lynas, to whom he has always considered himself much indebted for timely and valuable counsel and help given to him at that critical period of his life. His association with this godly friend contributed to the formation of his character, and the class-leader acted the part of an elder brother to the evangelist. Mr. Lynas, being a well-read man, was able to guide his young friend in his reading, and to help him in dealing with such intellectual difficulties as he had to face in common with other Christian young men. By his leader's advice, Thomas Cook joined the local Mission Band, which worked at a mission-room in the town. Commissioner Railton, of the Salvation Army, was a member of this Mission Band, and a candidate for the Wesleyan Methodist ministry; but his candidature was not encouraged by the Circuit quarterly meeting, and this was a great grief to the members of the Band. Some of the truest and most spiritually-minded men Mr. Cook has ever met were amongst the members of that humble organisation; and for his connection with it the evangelist has ever been, and must always continue to be, devoutly thankful. In that mission-room, where during two years no Sunday ever passed without some souls being brought to God, and by that Mission Band, Thomas Cook was trained for the work of the Christian ministry. During two years it was his custom to go nearly every Sunday morning with a blind local preacher through the slums of the town, exhorting the poor and vicious to forsake their sins. He and his companion would stand together at various street corners, and give brief addresses to the bystanders, and thus hold perhaps half-a-dozen services of a quarter of an hour's duration in as many different streets week by week. "Thou hast testified of Me in Jerusalem," said the Lord to His chosen vessel, St. Paul, "so must thou bear witness also at Rome." Mr. Cook has borne "witness" in many parts of the United Kingdom during the last ten years, but he began by testifying of Christ in his native town, and in the slums and alleys of that town. Happily, from the first he has had a deep conviction that a Christian is like a live coal, which can only be kept alight by setting other coals on fire, and thus has the gift of God been kept alive in his own soul.

Nor was his influence at home unfelt. Such is the frailty of even good men, that sometimes it is seen that whilst they are not unwilling to travel long distances to preach to strangers, or to submit to much inconvenience for the sake of being Sunday-school teachers, they cannot be induced to make the least effort to promote the spiritual welfare of their own families. Not so Thomas Cook. As we have seen, his mother was an earnest Christian, and it was no fault of hers that family prayer was neglected in her home. But such was the case prior to the conversion of Thomas, and one of the first things that he was able to do after that event was to establish a family altar in his home. Boy though he was, he led the devotions of the family, and he had the unspeakable happiness of knowing that his faithfulness in this respect contributed to promote the conversion of several of his brothers and sisters. " He that is faithful in that which is least, is faithful also in much."

In the previous chapter we intimated that we should have to refer to the late Dr. Punshon, and the time has now come to do so. Shortly after Mr. Cook's conversion, Dr. Punshon visited Middlesbrough for the purpose of addressing a public meeting. During the course of his speech the orator appealed to the young men who were present to offer themselves for the ministry. Thomas Cook's spirit was stirred in him; and although Dr. Punshon knew it not, the youth lifted up his heart to God in prayer, as he sat in the gallery of the Wesleyan Chapel, and said, " O God, if Thou canst make a minister of me, I offer myself for the work."

Instantly he knew that his offer was accepted, and he received the assurance that God would prepare him in His own way for the service to which that evening he was designated by Him who disposes of the lot which is " cast into the lap."

His education was defective for the office to which he aspired; and it was an instance of the goodness of God, who ordered his steps, that he was successful in obtaining a situation about this time as a pupil-teacher in a day-school. He was thus enabled to acquire a good deal of useful knowledge, which has since stood him in good stead.

He now became a local preacher. He took the

somewhat unusual course of asking a friend to mention his name at the local preachers' quarterly meeting, and was very naturally told that it was not customary for young men to take this honour unto themselves. But Thomas Cook's eye was single. He knew that he was called of God, "as was Aaron." He was burning with zeal for souls; the position of a local preacher appeared to offer suitable opportunities for indulging this passion; he was therefore anxious to secure it, and careless about conventionalities. When the eye is single, the whole body is full of light. I do not know that it would be wise to advise young men, as a general rule, to offer themselves for this work, as did Thomas Cook. Generally, it is better that faithful service rendered in obscurer paths should precede and awaken the call of the Church to more prominent appointments. Nevertheless, if a young man feels as Mr. Cook felt, if the Word of God is like fire in his bones, let him do what it is in his heart to do; he cannot do wrong.

The local preachers' meeting accepted Mr. Cook, and, having been a street preacher for some time, he now began to preach in the chapels.

His first service after coming on the plan was a peculiar one. Five persons formed the congregation; of these he took one with him; the chapel keeper and his wife were there as *ex officio* members; the remaining two were boys, who, unaware that they were taking part in any service of a historic character, retired before the young preacher had finished his sermon, not being interested in the discourse. There is a Methodist tradition to the effect that the late Samuel Coley once compared his own powers as a preacher with those of Morley Punshon, and declared that whilst Morley Punshon could excel him in preaching to three thousand persons, he could excel Morley Punshon in preaching to three individuals. The judgment was just: Samuel Coley could preach to three persons with infinite ease, and to their great edification; and we doubt not that Thomas Cook was able to preach to three persons with more freedom and reality than many preachers would have been able to do, because he spoke to them in a colloquial style out of the abundance of his heart. At the Christmas quarterly meeting, 1878, he was received as a fully accredited local preacher, after being examined in theology in the usual manner. During these days he was wise enough to buy Wesley's *Works*, and also Henry's peerless *Commentary*, of which Mr. Spurgeon says to students, "Buy it, even if you have to sell your coat to raise the necessary money." He likewise paid attention to another book which has had a rather long day, and which it is to be feared has marred as many preachers as it has made. This was Field's *Handbook of Theology*, which the writer once heard the late Dr. Osborn advise students not to read, unless they were precluded from studying better books. When Dr. Parker was preparing for the ministry, he studied Watson's *Institutes* under the guidance of a Wesleyan minister, to whose study he went daily at six o'clock in the morning for that purpose; and the writer has heard Dr. Parker express his thankfulness for the theological instruction he thus obtained. As it is hoped that these pages will be read by aspirants to the ministry, the writer ventures to commend the example of Dr. Parker to them, and to urge them not to be content with any *handbooks*, but to go to those well-heads from which the authors of handbooks themselves draw their supplies. Let the young student provide himself with Dr. Pope's *Works*, for example, and let him master them, in which case he will have reason to give thanks that there are theological writers for men as well as for children. Mr. Cook found much profit from reading Wesley's *Journals*, Fletcher's *Works*, Hunt's *Letters*, Arthur's *Tongue of Fire*, *Methodist Biography*, and some portions of Watson's *Institutes*. He was earnestly seeking entire sanctification, and this course of reading increased his desire for the blessing, and encouraged him to believe that his search would not be in vain.

During these days he received a letter from the Rev. J. H. Norton, which, as it is characteristic of the writer, and as suitable for other young preachers as it was for Mr. Cook, I will insert. Mr. Norton writes: "If you take a text, let it be a plain one. First, understand it yourself, then try to make those whom you address understand it. Be short; some speakers go over the same ground two or three times. Speak as a dying man to dying men. Let the people see that you love their souls, and wish to do them good. Pray much. Get what you have to say from the Word of God. Let all you say be sustained by 'Thus saith the Lord.' Do not fish for praise; and when persons give it, consider what their judgment is worth. When people blame you, and say you are wrong, ask them to set you right. There are some things you never can learn without the aid of books.

Paul was inspired, but he wanted 'the books and the parchments.' Redeem your time. Rise early. Do not attempt too much. Never be unemployed, but guard against busy idleness. Never forget that there is a time to be silent, as well as a time to speak. Many talk the most who have least to say. Connect all you do with God the Holy Ghost. He will help your infirmities. He will sanctify your nature, and comfort you under all your trials."

From the first it has pleased God to use Mr. Cook in the conversion of sinners. I wish to say, once for all, that if in these pages any praise seems to be accorded to Mr. Cook, it is not the writer's intention to increase Mr. Cook's fame.

Critics whose foible is omniscence may detect some sinister purpose in the book, and regard it as an illustration of the advertising spirit of the age. Candid readers, however, will accept the writer's assurance that no page has been, or will be, written to gratify "the last infirmity of noble minds." Who, then, is Thomas Cook but a minister, by whom many have believed, "even as the Lord gave to every man"? Our design is to show what the Lord has given him, and permitted him to do, "that, according as it is written, he that glorieth, let him glory in the Lord." During the two years that Mr. Cook was a local preacher, notwithstanding his youthfulness and inexperience, his ministry was richly blessed of God. His services were not confined to his own Church, but were freely given to the Primitive Methodists, the Salvation Army, and other denominations; and it rarely happened that even in those days he preached without having cause to rejoice over conversions, as may be gathered from the statement that during this period the names of three hundred persons were taken, all of whom publicly evinced a desire to flee from the wrath to come, at services that he conducted.

Surely this circumstance should be encouraging to local preachers. At the Nottingham Conference (1891), it was stated by a speaker that the interests of the work of God called for the renewed consecration of the ministers to the Lord Jesus Christ above everything else. It was also said by another speaker, that the local preachers needed to be aroused in order that rural England might be evangelised, and Methodism revived and extended. Why should not hundreds of local preachers be as successful in winning souls as Thomas Cook was in the days of which we now write? In thousands of villages the Sunday services are practically all conducted by lay preachers, and, therefore, if conversions are to take place in these rural chapels,—if the peasants are to be brought to God as well as the artisans,—the local preachers must be the instrument in the hands of God for achieving this purpose. In Wesleyan Methodism the local preachers are eight times as numerous as the travelling preachers, whilst, if we take the six branches of the Methodist Church, we find that the proportion is ten local preachers to one itinerant minister. Out of every seven Sunday services held in British Methodism, five are taken by local preachers, and 5500 of our Wesleyan pulpits are filled every Lord's day by these brethren. It should seem, therefore, that it is of the utmost importance that the local preachers, as well as the ministers, should renew their consecration, and should be full of faith and of the Holy Ghost. Their labours are often exhausting, their voluntary services are not always appreciated, and their discouragements are many. But when they taste the joy of saving souls from death, as Mr. Cook did when he belonged to their order, they are amply compensated for the hardships they endure, and they find it worth while to live "to administer bliss and salvation in Jesus' name." If the local preachers would read such books as Mr. Cook read when he was "on the plan,"—the *Memoirs of David Stoner*, Treffry's *Life of John Smith*, the *Life of David Brainerd*, Finney's *Autobiography*, and the other works previously mentioned,—they would catch the flame of holy zeal, and become inspired with a restless longing for the salvation of souls.

Mr. Cook preached nearly every Sunday during those two years, sometimes in adjacent towns. He spent a Sunday at Darlington with Mr. Joshua Dawson, and conducted services for the Salvation Army, the result being that he saw two hundred believers seeking purity of heart, and fourteen penitents seeking pardon. During his Christmas holidays in 1879, he held his first mission at Espland Hill, near Appleby. The Lord's presence was powerfully felt, and conversions took place. Amongst the converts of that mission were two old men, one being over seventy-nine years of age and the other over eighty Five years afterward, Mr. Cook found them walking in the fear of the Lord and the comfort of the Holy Ghost. One of them has since "died in faith;" the other still walks with God on earth. He also paid a visit to Newcastle-on-Tyne, where he held two or three most remarkable services. He addressed as many as four thousand people on that occasion, and witnessed such extraordinary manifestations of divine power that he was reminded of the occurrences that took place at times under the preaching of the Wesleys. The physical phenomena of which we read in Wesley's *Journals*, and which appear to some readers to be inexplicable, notwithstanding the tendency of the times to encourage the vagaries of the Psychical Research Society and the occultness of Theosophists, were, if not repeated, at least reproduced in some measure at these Newcastle services, and thus the mind of the young Evangelist was deeply impressed. About this time it pleased God to give Mr. Cook a remarkable dream. He dreamt that he was standing by a lake that was crowded with fish, and that he was casting in the nets, and enclosing a great multitude of fish, while a voice said to him, " I will make you a fisher of men." We who believe that Peter learnt, whilst he was "in a trance," that God had chosen from among the apostles "that the Gentiles by [his] mouth should hear the word of the gospel, and believe," shall have no difficulty in accepting the statement that, by this dream, God intended to show His young servant "things which must shortly come to pass." So Thomas Cook understood it, and the event has proved that his interpretation of the dream was correct. We have seen that Mr. Cook was led early, in his Christian life, to seek the blessing of entire sanctification. Having noticed in his reading that all the great evangelists of Methodism had enjoyed a Pentecost in their lives, and that the reception of this great blessing brought such increased power for service that it inaugurated a new era in their religious life, Mr. Cook was prompted to seek for himself this enduement of power. In course of time he received the "second blessing," as our fathers used to term it, which altered his Christian life almost as much as the "first blessing" altered his natural life; and to this auspicious event he attributes, more than to any other occurrence since his conversion, the great usefulness of his ministry. As he regards the finding of this inestimable blessing as the main part of his preparation for the work which lay before him, the reader will be glad to have the opportunity of learning from Mr. Cook himself what was the nature of the blessing which he then received, and what was the effect which it produced upon his life and ministry. I therefore subjoin the following account which Mr. Cook has published in a small tract, entitled, *Thomas Cook's Experience:*—

"My conversation was so clear and satisfactory that I could never doubt its reality. Need I say it was an eventful period in my history when I first realised God's pardoning mercy, and received the assurance of His favour? The beginnings of this life of loyalty and love I shall never forget. It seems but as yesterday, though ten years have now passed since the love of God was shed abroad in my heart, and I was reconciled to God, who loved me, even me. It was a change as from death unto life. A new fountain of joys was at once opened in my heart, so exceedingly precious and sweet as to utterly extinguish all desire for that which I had called pleasure before. All my fears of death, judgment, and hell were fully swept away, and I could do nothing but praise God continually. My tastes, desires, and impulses were all changed; 'all things became new.' I was truly a new creature, and seemed to be in a new world.

"With such experiences, is it any wonder I imagined the work of moral renovation was perfected, that sin was not only forgiven, but fully expelled from my soul? But soon I discovered my mistake. My highly-wrought emotions subsided, and petty annoyances of life chafed, the temptations of the devil assailed; and then I found out, as pride, envy, unbelief, self-will, and other forms of heart-sin stirred within me, that much needed to be done before I could be 'meet for the inheritance of the saints in light.' The 'old man' was bound, but not cast out; the disease was modified, but not eradicated; sin was suspended, but not fully destroyed. True, sin was stunned and deadened and held in check by grace; its power was broken, but its pollution continued. It did not reign, but it existed, making its presence felt in a constant 'bent to sinning,' and at times a painful sense of duality contrasting most strikingly with the sweet feeling of oneness with Christ I now experience. There were foes within as well as without; some of the Canaanites remained, and were thorns in my side and pricks in my eyes; the flesh and spirit were in a state of antagonism, which I saw to be manifestly only a temporary position—one or the other must eventually conquer; the light was mingled with darkness, and love with its opposites.

"How many headaches and heartaches I had in struggling with my bosom foes no language can describe. All the time I was enjoying sweet fellowship with Christ, was blessedly conscious of acceptance in Him, was an earnest worker in the Lord's vineyard, and would rather have died then wilfully sinned against Him. But though I never was a backslider in the ordinary sense, my Christian life was unsatisfactory, at least to myself. There was much of vacillation about it, sinning and repenting, advancing and retrograding, swinging like a pendulum between God and the world. At times I was all earnestness, zeal, and fervour; then comparatively cold, careless, and indifferent. My experience was full of fits and starts, changeable and uneven. I was conscious also of a mighty want; there seemed a vacuum in my nature which grace had not filled, a strange sense of need, which I cannot describe, but which all who love the Lord Jesus with less than perfect love will understand. My efforts to save men were unabated, but no adequate results followed. I fear now that to furnish subject-food for self-worship was the great end in much that I did, and not the glory of Jesus.

"For three years this half-and-half sort of life continued, when I was so dissatisfied that I felt, unless I had something better, I could not go on any longer. Reading Methodist biographies about this time stirred my heart, and filled me with hope for better things. I thought what God had done for others He could do for me; and an inexpressible longing possessed me to enjoy the fulness of which they spoke. I began at once to seek it, determined to give God no rest until I was sanctified wholly. The more earnestly I sought, the worse I seemed to become. What a view I had of the sinfulness of my own heart! I saw what a charnel-house it was — a depth of depravity there which would once have utterly paralysed my faith and extinguished my hope. I then apprehended the goodness of God in not revealing to me my need of cleansing when I sought forgiveness. It was enough that I should realise my guilt, and exposure to the pangs of the second death, when I came to God at first. Had I then seen my own heart sin as I saw it afterwards, I believe I should have despaired in view of the difficulties, so God's revelation of my need was tempered in mercy until I had strength enough to receive it. On the same principle, God did not lead Israel from Egypt to Canaan by the shortest route, but, lest they should faint in the presence of their enemies, He led them by a way more roundabout. It was in my case very similar to that of Professor Upham, 'the remains of every form of internal opposition to God appeared to be centred in one point— selfishness.' I had once prayed to be saved from hell, but prayer to be saved from *myself* now was immeasurably more fervent. How I struggled and wrestled for the victory I shall never be able to tell, but sin and self die hard.

"From experiences I had read and listened to, I imagined it would be all gladness entering into this rest, but I found it a different process. The way was through the Garden and by the Cross; I had to learn the hard lesson that every victory is gained by surrender, and that the place of life is the place of death. Only from the ashes of a dead Jacob can the prevailing Israel arise. I saw it all clearly enough: that before there could be a full and glorious resurrection to spiritual life and blessedness, there must first be a complete death of self—my hands must be empty if

I would grasp a whole Christ. Again and again I searched my heart and surrendered, praying all the while that any idol might be uncovered of which I was unconscious—that the Holy Spirit would make demand after demand, until self was exhausted. Perhaps my reputation was the last thing laid on the altar. How concerned I used to be for the good opinion of my fellow-mortals, instead of seeking the honour that comes from God only! But I see now, that I never had any reputation until I gave it to God. Blessed paradox, 'He that loseth his life for My sake shall save it;' and in all other matters this is equally true. Acting upon the advice of one deeply experienced in divine things, I wrote upon paper the several items included, as well as the obligations assumed, in the complete consecration of myself to God. I did this to secure definiteness of surrender.

"At last I felt sure, so far as I knew it (and we are not responsible for what we do not know), upon all I had I could honestly inscribe 'sacred to Jesus.' The language of my soul was, 'None of self, and all of Thee.' But still the Lord tarried. Why did He not come and fill His temple? I saw afterwards it was because I did not receive Him by simple faith. In consecration we give all, by faith we take all; and the one is as essential as the other. I had received justification by faith, but was seeking sanctification by works. What strugglings and wrestlings and tears I might have been saved had I known the simple way of faith then as I do now! But I had no one to help me.

"Some months passed, during which I was at times almost in a state of despair; but my extremity was

God's opportunity. At this very juncture, when I felt I must die unless I received the grace, Mr. Joshua Dawson came to our town, and proclaimed 'full salvation' to be a present duty and privilege. There was no disputing his teaching: if by faith, it must be a present experience. Faith cannot be otherwise than an instantaneous operation. It was like a revelation from heaven to me; and I rejoiced in hope, though not in actual possession of the fulness during his visit. Some friends entered into the rest before he left, but, greatly to my disappointment, I did not. Instead of receiving Christ as my Saviour to the uttermost in the absence of all feeling, I waited for some wondrous emotion, some great exaltation of soul. In fact, I was seeking the experience of another friend, who had been prostrated under the weight of glory which fell upon him as he wrestled for the blessing. How many seekers make this same mistake! They forget that in all God's works is beautiful variety; and in the spiritual world this is as true as in the natural world. He scarcely ever deals with two persons alike. I had set the Lord a plan to work by, and was disappointed. Instead of in the mighty torrent, God spoke to me in the 'still small voice.' I saw my blunder afterwards, and was willing to be blessed in God's own way—with or without emotion. It was then—oh, glory to His name!—He spoke to me the second time, 'Be clean.'

"The circumstances were as follows:—A few friends who had received 'full salvation' during Mr. Dawson's visit decided to meet together week by week, to encourage each other in the way and assist those who might be seeking the experience. It was at the first meeting where the Lord met me. After listening to their experiences, I could bear no longer, but asked them to begin at once to pray that I might enter in. I fell upon my knees, with the determination not to rise again until my request was granted. The passage, ' If we walk in the light, as He is in the light, we have fellowship one with another; and the blood of Jesus Christ, His Son, cleanseth us from all sin,' was instantly applied to my heart, and with such power as I had never felt before. What a fulness of meaning I saw in the words! Was I walking in the light? Truthfully I could answer, 'Yes, Lord; so far as I know Thy will I am doing it, and will do it, by Thy grace helping me.' I then saw that the passage was not so much a promise as a plain declaration. If I walked in light, the full cleansing from sin was my heritage; and all I had to do was to immediately claim it. Without a moment's hesitation I did so, and cried out at the top of my voice, ' I claim the blessing now.' My friends then began to sing,—

" ' 'Tis done ! Thou dost this moment save,
With full salvation bless ;
Redemption through Thy blood I have,
And spotless love and peace.'

" While they sang, the refining fire came down and went through my heart,—searching, probing, melting, burning, filling all its chambers with light, and hallowing my whole heart to God. Oh the indescribable sweetness of that moment! All words fail to express the blessedness of the spiritual manifestation of Jesus as my Saviour from all sin. My heart warms as I write at the remembrance of the event which transcends all others in my religious history. It was not so much ecstatic emotion I experienced as an unspeakable peace—'God's love swallowed me up.' For a few moments 'all its waves and billows rolled over me.' So much afraid was I lest I should lose the delightful sense of the Saviour's presence, that I wished those with me not to speak or disturb me; I wanted to dwell in silence, as my heart was filled with love and gratitude to God.

"I need not say the reception of this grace proved an era in my religious life. Six beautiful years have passed away since then. But no words can ever express the complete satisfaction I have in Christ: the sweet sense of rest in His hallowing presence from all worry and care; the ease and joy of His service—not 'I must' now, but 'I may;' the delight I find in prayer and praise; the increased preciousness and fulness of meaning I see in the Scriptures; and the clear and indubitable witness of cleansing through the blood of Jesus. Spurgeon says there is a point in grace as much above the ordinary Christian as the ordinary Christian is above the worldling. Surely this is it—to live in the 'Heavenlies,' 'where dwells the Lord our righteousness,' and keeps His own in perfect peace and everlasting rest. At least the transformation in my experience has been as great. How I wish I could tell of the sweetness, and richness, and indescribable blessedness of this life of perfect love! I cannot tell the story; but I cannot let it alone. Oh for a thousand tongues to proclaim Jesus to men,—the mighty Saviour who is able to save them to the uttermost who come unto God by Him! Reader, will you join us and help to spread the sacred flame?

" ' In blessing Thee with grateful songs
  My happy life shall glide away :
The praise that to Thy name belongs
  Hourly with lifted hands I'll pay.

Abundant sweetness, while I sing
  Thy love, my ravish'd heart o'erflows ;
Secure in Thee, my God and King,
  Of glory that no period knows.' "

CHAPTER IV

A LAY EVANGELIST.

IT was deeply impressed upon Mr. Cook's mind that he was called of God to the Christian ministry. He was at that time, as we have seen, engaged as a day-school teacher. He had the opportunity of entering Westminster Training College, and was disposed to think that he could eventually succeed in that profession. He did not therefore look towards the Christian ministry for the reason that induced a certain eminent lawyer once to turn his eyes in that direction, of whom his biographer naïvely says, that "his prospects were at one time so gloomy that he had serious thoughts of taking holy orders." Mr. Cook's prospects were not "gloomy," but "necessity was laid upon" him; yea, he felt that "woe was unto him" if he preached not the gospel; and, therefore, as entering Westminster Training College would have involved a pledge that he would devote a number of years to the work of teaching, he declined the proposal, and awaited the further call of God, which he was convinced would soon come. He examined his motives, and was convinced that ambition had nothing to do with his decision. At the same time, he was deterred from offering himself for the ministry by a feeling of unfitness for the work.

Overtures were made to him by the representatives of other Churches, who desired him to enter their ranks, but he dwelt among his own people, and he therefore did not entertain any offer that came to him from outside of Wesleyan Methodism. In the year 1880 he was nominated as a candidate for the Wesleyan ministry, in the quarterly meeting of the Middlesbrough Circuit, by the Rev. Philip Fowler, and, somewhat to his surprise, the nomination was unanimously approved.

His preaching had excited a little opposition. He had aimed at the immediate salvation of his hearers, and he had not scrupled to use means to further this end which were not approved of all. Moreover, he had taught the doctrine of entire sanctification, and urged his hearers to seek the blessing; and he had witnessed to the enjoyment of it in his own experience. This also caused some difference of opinion. From Wesley's day to the times of the Southport Conventions, it has been impossible to proclaim the full privileges of the children of God without exciting opposition, and the opposition usually comes from one's own household. However, Thomas Cook was sent to the district meeting, with the imprimatur of his own Circuit quarterly meeting, as a candidate for the ministry Having to preach "a trial sermon," prior to the district meeting, before three ministers, he took occasion to bear witness to the truth of full salvation, and thereby caused a little surprise, for he was but a boy. At the district meeting he was examined in theology by the Rev. Edward Watson, and again he declared, in the presence of the ministers, that the blood of Jesus Christ cleansed him from all sin. All candidates for the Wesleyan Methodist ministry are required to be seekers after this great blessing, and are distinctly asked whether such is the case; and yet—such is the frailty of human nature—if any candidate affirms that he has found the "pearl which others spurn," his confession creates surprise, and sometimes opposition.[1] Thus, at the close of the Chairman's examination, a member of the District Committee exercised his right to ask the candidate a few questions on his own account. He inquired if Mr. Cook still had reason to use the Lord's Prayer, and was told in reply that the candidate continued to do so, chiefly because he had learnt to distinguish between trespasses and sins. I am not sure that the young theologian was right in the distinction which he drew; for although the version of the Lord's Prayer which we use, and which we have learnt from the Book of Common Prayer, gives the word "trespasses," the Gospels give the words "debts" and "sins." However, the District Committee was assured when it heard that, for whatever reason, Mr. Cook had not got beyond the Lord's Prayer. He was then asked to explain the difference between sanctification and regeneration, and did so to the satisfaction of the meeting. Finally, he was asked to explain the difference between the love of God which is characteristic of the regenerated man, and that which is characteristic of the sanctified man.

The Chairman, however, interposed, remarking that the candidate had not been a student of theology for forty years, and should not be unduly pressed.

It should seem that the district meeting was satis-

---

[1] See "Notices of my Life and Times," by the Rev. Dr. Gregory, in the *Wesleyan Methodist Magazine* for November 1891, where the Connexional Editor describes a somewhat similar experience.

fied with the examination, for the marks given were not amiss; but the sermon he preached, and which was reported upon in the usual way, was not deemed satisfactory, and received low marks.

It will be remembered that the sermon bore witness to the doctrine of entire sanctification; and as the preacher pressed the blessing upon his hearers, and at the close of the service urged them to come forward to the communion rail and seek it as a definite experience, some displeasure was excited. It was also said that the sermon was "too colloquial;" and the soft impeachment cannot be denied, for the youth was but twenty years of age, and had only paid attention for a short time to literature and composition.

However, the District Committee recommended him to the Conference, and thus discharged its duty.

Twice he had now passed the sieve; but as candidates for the Wesleyan ministry are invariably riddled over three times, he had another and more severe ordeal to pass before he could be accepted by the Conference. In July he had to appear before a committee appointed by the Conference for the purpose, and to satisfy the members of it that his preaching and knowledge of theology were sufficient to justify his acceptance. It is characteristic of Thomas Cook that when he had appeared before the committee, and was waiting in another room with his fellow-candidates to know the result, he utilised the time by relating to the young men his experience of full salvation. To the credit of these young men it must be said, that they did not resent this action on the part of one of the youngest of their number, as David's brothers resented his appearance on the battle-field, when Eliab said to him, " I know thy pride, and the naughtiness of thine heart." On the contrary, they thanked him for his testimony, and some promised that they never would rest until they shared his glorious experience. Subsequent events proved that at least one or two of those young men were profoundly and permanently impressed by that episode, which may perhaps be regarded as an illustration of what St. Paul means when he bids the preacher to be "instant" out of season as well as in season.

It so happened that the number of candidates was that year in excess of the demand, and for this reason chiefly his offer was not accepted, and the July Committee did not recommend him to the Conference. Others were, of course, declined as well, and some of them were deeply distressed at their rejection. But Thomas Cook was not distressed in the least, for he knew that he was in his heavenly Father's hands, and that all would be overruled for good. He was, however, grieved, because, as it seemed to him, some of the candidates who apparently were most devoted to God were declined; and one of these, at all events, sorrowed more for the rejection of Thomas Cook than for his own. This young man, as was afterwards ascertained, went down to breakfast in tears soon after his return home, and when his mother gently chided him for weeping over his failure, as she supposed, he told her that he was not grieving on account of his own rejection, but on account of Thomas Cook; "for," said he, " what is to become of Methodism if candidates like Thomas Cook are declined?"

That the July Committee erred in judgment when they declined Mr. Cook's offer, would now be admitted probably by every minister who sat upon it; and if they went astray in one case, it is possible they did so in others. But when this is stated, it is only said that "the best of men are but men at the best," and that, although actuated by the purest motives, they are liable to err.

Infallible critics will be ready to denounce the unwisdom of the committee, but we are content to point the moral of the story. To admit unworthy or inefficient men into the ministry is to strike with paralysis the Church of Christ; while to exclude from the ministry men whom God has called, is to inflict almost as great an injury upon the Church. Those, therefore, who are called upon to decide whether candidates shall be accepted or declined, do well to address themselves to their solemn duties after a period of fasting and prayer.

After his rejection, Mr. Cook continued to preach as before, preaching always on the Lord's day, and sometimes on week evenings, and nearly always rejoicing over visible fruit. In October 1880 he held a mission at New Marske with Mr. Davidson, now the Rev. Edward Davidson, one of Mr. Cook's colleagues, and a Connexional evangelist. Mr. Cook and Mr. Davidson were brought up as boys together, and hitherto they have not been divided. They both belong by birth to a preaching part of the Connexion, the district from which they came having given Methodism many preachers, and having sent eight men to the ministry recently, who are all at the time of writing students in the Wesleyan Theological Colleges. The mission at New Marske was blessed; the young Evangelists took alternate services; and about thirty or forty converts were the visible results of the preachers' labours.

In November 1880, the Rev. Joseph Bush, then

the chairman of the Halifax and Bradford District, having heard, through the late Rev Alexander Macaulay, of the success of Mr. Cook's local ministry, wrote to Mr. Cook, and offered him the appointment of lay evangelist to his district. Mr. Cook recognised the hand of God in the offer, and accepted it at once, and began work in that capacity in the Halifax and Bradford District on the 21st of November 1880.

The present writer was travelling in one of the Bradford Circuits at the time, and he has a distinct recollection of the commencement of Mr. Cook's district work. He remembers what was said in the District meeting about Mr. Cook's age, and preaching, and rejection by the July Committee, as well as what was said about his devotion and the great success which God was giving him in his own Circuit and neighbourhood. It cannot be said that he entered on his District work with great advantages. His youth was a stumbling-block to some, and his failure at the "July Committee" somewhat damaged him. Howbeit, "the Lord seeth not as man seeth," for no sooner did this youth of a ruddy countenance begin to preach than the Lord began to confirm the word, and signs and wonders were wrought by the name of His holy Child Jesus. He was sent, as the writer well remembers, to some of the smallest and apparently most unfruitful places in the District—to small struggling Circuits where revivals were unknown excepting by tradition; he was also sent to the largest and most influential places. But it mattered not where he went; the same report reached us from every Circuit which he visited, and it was to this effect, that unusually large congregations had been gathered

D

together, sometimes crowded congregations, and that great numbers of men and women had been converted to God.

Mr. Cook began his work as a District lay evangelist in the Bradford (Windhill) Circuit. His methods were new; others have now adopted them, and we are familiar with them; and, moreover, they have been justified by success. God has let it be known that Thomas Cook is His servant, and that he has done all these things at His word, and hence opposition has ceased. But when he first commenced, his plans met with some disfavour. As his aims and methods will be dealt with in a subsequent chapter, it need only be said here that, from the first, he has been accustomed to invite any of his hearers who have been impressed by the Word to rise in their places, that they might have the benefit of the prayers of the congregation. He then usually commends the persons who respond to his invitation to God in prayer, after which he directs them to repair to the inquiry-rooms, in order that experienced Christians may do for them what Aquila and Priscilla did for Apollos when he was an inquirer, and they "expounded unto him the way of God more perfectly." Generally, there is not much opportunity in Mr. Cook's after-meetings for persons to engage in public prayer, nor is there any going about from pew to pew to speak to individuals. Often all the burden of the public service rests upont he evangelist, the whole of "the workers" being directed to go to the inquiry-rooms, and the penitents all being sent there, instead of being directed to kneel at the communion rail, as was the custom prior to the days of the Connexional evangelists. It will thus be seen that Mr. Cook's methods were contrary to the traditions of the elders; and as he was but one-and-twenty when he introduced them into Methodism, it is not surprising that he had to encounter some opposition. Had his methods failed, they must have been abandoned; but he had a firm conviction that they were the best he could adopt, and therefore he held fast to them, and God graciously sanctioned them with an abundant blessing. Each evening the congregation, at that first mission in the Bradford District, increased, and increased spontaneously. That is to say, no special means were used to attract congregations, but the news was blazed abroad that sinners were being converted, and many said in effect to the mission preacher: "We will go with you, for we have heard that God is with you." On the evening of the second Lord's day forty adults entered the inquiry-rooms.

As a rule, Mr. Cook's services are marked by stillness and the absence of excitement; but exciting incidents have always occurred in his missions, and the element of romance has never been lacking. Thus, at this first mission, a man walked quickly down the aisle at one of the services and cried lustily to God for mercy. When he reached the rail he fell down on the floor, and in much distress audibly exclaimed, "Lord, save me." One of the helpers essayed to comfort him; but the penitent, supposing that the helper intended to speak to him on some other subject, said: "Get away, man, I have no time to talk; I want to be saved. My father is in heaven, and I wish to go there too." He was the son of a godly class-leader who had died a few weeks before the mission was held, and he did not cry out of the depths in vain. He is now an earnest Christian, and one of the best, as well as one of the first, fruits of Mr. Cook's ministry.

Work of this kind has always been opposed and disparaged. The ungodly sneer at it, and seek to discredit the agents of it. The motives of Mr. Moody were impugned when he was carrying on his great work in these islands; and of General Booth it has often been said, by those who love to make a lie, that he and his family have made "a good thing" out of the Salvation Army These palpable calumnies are easy to understand; for "if they have called the Master of the house Beelzebub, how much more shall they call them of His household?" It is not, however, easy to understand why Christian people, and sometimes even ministers of religion, make light of the results of evangelistic services. Let the following weighty words of the Rev. W Arthur be pondered by all whom they concern:—

"A more pitiable thing cannot be, than to see a man who, himself destitute of ministerial power, not only is unconscious how miserable a creature he is, but is even ready to make light of the usefulness of others; and, in his ordinary conversation, to set down those whom the Lord honours as the instruments of converting sinners, below what he calls "intellectual" men, who deal out dainties from the pulpit, but do no work that will live when they are dead.
In the great day how differently will the two men appear—the one whose humble labour has been the means of converting servant-maids, and the one

whose envy and whose wit were vented in making light of the work."

The first mission which Mr. Cook held as a lay evangelist was discredited by unbelievers, as no doubt his last mission was. Fifteen months after the close of the Windhill Mission, a friend reported to Mr. Cook that he had been told by an official that he did not think that there were then three persons in the Windhill Society who were brought to God at that mission. Had this been so, the mission could not justly have been pronounced a failure on this account, for the fruits of a mission are never given wholly to any one Society, nor to any one Circuit, nor indeed to any one Church. As it was, however, the statement was proved to be without foundation. One of the leaders of the Society visited the Windhill classes with a view to investigate the statement, and he was able to report that sixty-four persons were actually meeting in class at that time who were all the fruits of the mission held eighteen months before. The names of those persons and of their leaders are now before me, in a document prepared by the leader who made the inquiry, and which happens to have been preserved; and had the scope of the inquiry been enlarged, and made to embrace the other Societies in the Circuit and the sister Churches in the town, there is reason to believe that it would have been proved that the abiding fruit of that mission was more considerable than the figures just quoted indicate.

The evangelist's boyish appearance in those days created no little surprise. "Bless the dear lad," an old lady was heard to exclaim when he ascended the pulpit steps during one of his early missions; and similar exclamations were often made. Sometimes a humorous incident would happen. Thus, when Mr. Cook went to a Circuit in the Bradford District known to the writer, to conduct a mission, he was met at the railway station by a good man, who was so struck by the evangelist's youthfulness that he involuntarily made a hole in his manners. Eyeing the preacher from head to foot, the honest Yorkshireman asked, "Are *you* the man?" With becoming meekness Thomas Cook pleaded guilty, and thereupon the disappointed representative of the Circuit said, "Come on, I'm afraid we shall not have much done." During this period Mr. Cook held a mission in the Manningham Circuit, Bradford, which was, all things considered, perhaps as remarkable for results as any mission he has since conducted. Services were held in four of the chapels in the Circuit, and altogether not less than five hundred persons professed to find peace with God. The work in St. John's Chapel in that Circuit was, to many, a surprise, and it remains a pleasant and an inspiring recollection. The reader must know that St. John's Chapel, Manningham, is one of the handsomest structures in British Methodism, the premises having cost about twenty thousand pounds. There is a lurking suspicion in the minds of some excellent people that costly and splendid chapels do not permit of successful spiritual work being done within their walls. If this suspicion is well grounded the Connexion ought to know it, and to resolve to build no more magnificent sanctuaries as long as the moon endures. Some of the devout Bradford Methodists really doubted whether it was within the range of possibility for conversions to take place in this ornate church, with its impressive liturgical service and its male choir robed in black gowns. The writer has heard it said by Bradford Methodists, who prefer mission halls to Gothic chapels, that the twenty thousand pounds which these premises cost were lying idle, and would not yield any return to the Circuit, which had raised that large sum and expended it for the purpose of spreading the gospel. Nevertheless, as soon as Mr. Cook began his mission in St. John's Chapel, the power of the Lord was displayed, and neither Gothic architecture, nor the use of the liturgy, nor the gowns of the choir, prevented the Spirit of the Lord from working amongst the congregation, and adding to the Society many "who were being saved." At one of the after-meetings a Methodist, who belonged to an adjacent Circuit, engaged in prayer, and deemed it right to intersperse his petitions with these observations: "I said I would never come into this place until I heard of souls being saved in it; and now, Lord, that a revival has begun, I have come to pray Thee to carry it on."

Some three years after the close of this mission, Mr. Cook was standing near the building, and wondering how the converts of the mission were prospering, when a lady accosted him, and told him that she was one of the fruits of the mission, her brother was another, and her two sisters and mother were also amongst them. Thus five members of one family had been brought to God during the mission, and they were then holding fast what they had received. Another of the converts of the same mission has been working in the East End of London with the Rev. Peter Thompson for some time.

Surely there is no reason, in the nature of the case, why conversions should not occur as frequently in spacious and elegant suburban chapels as in plain structures and crowded mission halls. And yet it cannot be denied that services in these superb buildings bear no such fruit. Does it not lie upon those who conduct such services to explain this circumstance?

The work of this period was extensive as well as deep, as may be gathered from the fact that during twenty weeks, two thousand adults entered the inquiry-rooms in the various missions that Mr. Cook conducted. Disappointment is often felt because the net result of a mission to the particular Society under whose auspices it is held is not so large as it was expected to be. To some extent disappointment is inevitable, for "the kingdom of heaven is like unto a net that was cast into the sea, *and gathered of every kind.*" But our disappointment would be less, if we remembered that mission services always enrich many Churches besides the one in connection with which they are held. When our fathers asked themselves what the design of God was in the rise of Methodism, they answered, "To reform the nation, and especially the Church, by spreading scriptural holiness over the land." Since, therefore, our object is not to swell the number of our adherents, and thus build up a huge sect, we ought not to overlook the benefit that our missions confer on sister Churches. I have before me a statement in the handwriting of the Rev. Marshall Hartley, dated May 10th, 1881, which gives what he calls a "Summary of our Results," and as it refers to a mission which Mr. Cook held during the period now under review, and is typical of all his missions, I will trouble the reader with the figures, merely premising that they refer to a mission held in Richmond Terrace Chapel, Bradford, of which Mr. Hartley then had charge. Six hundred and eight converts are accounted for in the following way :—

Wesleyans,	362
Church of England,	72
Independents,	54
Baptists,	43
Primitives,	28
Methodist Free Church,	14
Reformers,	11
New Connexion,	7
Presbyterians, Quakers, and Salvation Army,	8
From other towns,	9
Total,	608

Mr. Hartley adds to his statement the words, "Glory to God in the highest."

Mr. Moody gloried in the unsectarian character of his work in this country, and persistently refused to identify himself with any particular Church, because he wished to "make disciples of all nations," and not to make denominationalists of any nation. When he was pressed to say of what persuasion he was, he replied, "Of St. Paul's, who was persuaded that He was able to keep that which he had committed to Him." Mr. Cook is identified with a particular Church, and, like all Wesleyan ministers, would fain increase the membership of his own denomination. But it is no disparagement of his work to say that from the very first it has greatly enriched all the Churches.

Mr. Cook's second year in the Halifax and Bradford District was more remarkable than the first. He visited more of the larger Circuits, and the work assumed wider proportions. One of the first missions of the second year was held in the Rhodes Street Chapel, Halifax. An abundant blessing rested upon the services, some hundreds of persons professing conversion as the result of them. Among the converts was one whose story is full of interest and pathos. He is a native of Halifax, an old Sunday-school scholar, the son of irreligious persons, and he was at the time of his conversion about twenty-three years old. When he reached adolescence, like thousands of others, he turned his back on the Sunday school and the house of God, and became addicted to the vices of gambling, clog dancing in public-houses, and drunkenness. During the week preceding the Sunday on which he attended the mission, he drank heavily, getting drunk, and sober and drunk again on the same day more than once, so that when the Lord's day came, he was worn out with his excesses. The Wesleyan Chapel being too small for the Sunday services, the Drill Hall was taken, and news of this reaching the young fellow, he suggested to the girl whom he was courting that they should go in the evening to the service. A collection was to be made for the Sunday school, and the young man gave the girl sixpence wherewith to get two threepenny pieces, that when that part of the ceremony was reached they might both acquit themselves with propriety.

Accordingly, they went to the service, and although it might have been supposed that he was soddened with drink, he was deeply convicted of sin, and remained to the after-meeting. When the evangelist urged his hearers to immediate decision, this young man trembled from head to foot, and, as he afterwards expressed it, "hell seemed up in arms to prevent him from going forward as a penitent." But when Mr. Cook exhorted those who were convinced of sin to honour God by coming out boldly, and said that if they did so God would honour them, he jumped to his feet and walked to the inquiry-room. There he found peace with God. Being a lamplighter, he was obliged to leave early to go on duty. When he reached his lodgings he knelt down and said, "Lord, Thou hast brought me out before all yon' people, now make me real for Thee." The prayer was answered. For twelve months afterwards he shared his room with a man who denied the existence of God, and who at times would stamp and rave and tell the convert that his conversion was only a delusion. But he would reply, "You and I used to swear, and fight, and gamble, but you don't find me doing such things now. I read my Bible, I pray, I go to chapel and Sunday school instead of the public-house, and these things are not delusions."

At the time of his conversion he was heavily in debt, the clothes he wore not being paid for, and many ale-shots standing against him in the public-houses. But by the blessing of God upon his industry, he succeeded in paying all his debts. The young woman to whom he was engaged was converted also, and, twelve months after the mission, Mr. Cook had the pleasure of marrying them. Since then the convert has done much useful work, and has himself led not a few to Christ. Many who were brought to

God at that mission "have fallen asleep." Amongst this number was a young woman who died in 1882. Her Christian life was short, but it matured quickly. During her illness she was continually praising God for the blessing received during the mission. A friend brought her a photograph of Mr. Cook, which she kissed and then handed to her mother, asking her mother to keep it for her sake. She then immediately lost consciousness, and gradually sank until she languished into life. She also will be amongst the sheaves which the reaper will bring with him when he comes again rejoicing.

Nothing is so interesting as mission work. People who are fond of romance may have their taste fully gratified if only they will throw themselves heartily into God's service, and instead of being content to be ankle-deep in it, will take "a header," and plunge into it. The incident just narrated is a pathetic one, but humorous stories occur as frequently in the experience of an evangelist as pathetic incidents.

During Mr. Cook's visit to the Halifax Circuits in those days, a number of young fellows, neither men nor boys, joined themselves into a band with the intention of making sport and mischief by opposing the mission. As the mission band marched down the street, this "skeleton band" would walk in the rear of them, led by a man who imitated the Salvation Army, and walked backwards. One evening the Evangelist thought he would test their mettle, and being in nothing terrified by his adversaries, he left his own company and wended his steps towards the enemy. When these valorous youths saw the young preacher coming towards them, they halted suddenly, and waited to see whether he or they had most courage. As soon as they discovered that he was bent on getting to close quarters, every mother's son took to his heels and fled. The skeleton band was about thirty strong on that occasion, and to see all these brave hobbledehoys fleeing when no man was pursuing them was a pleasant sight to those who love honest laughter as they love sunlight.

The reader has doubtless often sung,—

> "Many giants, great and tall,
> Stalking through the land,
> Headlong to the earth would fall
> If met by Daniel's band."

An authentic story like this will enable the reader to give credence to the poet's fancy; for if thirty giants, great and tall, fled when confronted by *one* who dared to be a Daniel, it is conceivable that "Daniel's band" might do great things. "Deal courageously, and the Lord shall be with the good."

But the better part of the story is yet untold. That evening the skeleton band came in a body to the mission service, attracted perhaps by the preacher's "pluck," for young fellows like these know a *man* when they see one. The evangelist did what he seldom does, and what should not be done excepting under divine impulse—he singled out the leader of the band, and told him he would be largely responsible for the fate of the others, and pleaded with him to forsake his way. The word was not spoken in vain. He and several of his companions sought salvation that night, and by the time the mission was over nearly all the members of that band were avowed

Christians. Another interesting episode in this mission was the conversion of a policeman. Some idea may be gathered of the size of the congregations that came to Mr. Cook's services in those days, from the fact that it was necessary to have a policeman at the chapel door to keep order. The writer himself has conducted mission services in that county when no such precaution was necessary, and possibly the reader may know of missions which have been held at which the mission preacher would have been glad to have made the same arrangement, if only it had been called for by the exigencies of the work.

Mr. Cook gave the constable half-a-crown for his trouble, and instructed him to remain during the service in the chapel-porch. Whilst standing in the vestibule the officer heard enough of the Word of God to convince him of sin, and when he was released from "duty" he went home, doffed his uniform, and returned to the after-meeting in time to seek and find that night peace with God. Having thus unexpectedly found the kingdom of heaven, which is like treasure hid in a field, "for joy thereof" he returned the half-crown to the preacher who had "sown unto [him] spiritual things." Thus is God found of them that sought Him not.

A successful mission followed at Linthwaite, near Huddersfield, at the close of which the converts were publicly recognised as members of the Wesleyan Methodist Church. The Leaders' Meeting passed a resolution in which they recorded their thankfulness for the blessing vouchsafed to their Society.

The Low Moor Circuit, Bradford, was also the scene of a wonderful visitation. As many as a hundred persons entered the inquiry-rooms on the same evening more than once during that mission. The singing-band, which often is a sign of poverty, if not a flag of distress, would often be five hundred strong, and its "marches" were characterised by an enthusiasm and a determination that presaged victory. So great were the crowds that it was impossible to accommodate them in the chapel, and overflow meetings were held, which was a circumstance without precedent in the history of local Methodism. Readers know how difficult it usually is to get good congregations on week evenings for evangelistic services, but at Low Moor on that occasion the tables were turned, and the difficulty was to accommodate the people who clamoured for admission, and who seemed disposed to mob the young preacher in their eagerness to hear the Word of life from his lips. And yet nothing could have been simpler than Mr. Cook's preaching. Mr. Spurgeon has somewhere said that he can preach nothing but the gospel, because he knows nothing else; and Mr. Cook could have said the same with more truth when he was at Low Moor. Nor were the services made attractive by orchestral music or by the singing of solos. The preacher did not attract in order to convert, but he attracted by converting. His God-given converting power was his sole attraction. How true are these sentences from the *Tongue of Fire*: "The converting power is also the Church's great attraction. It is true that some would attract men by ceremonies, or talent, or the charms of music or architecture—attract them that they may convert them; whereas the true order is, Convert, that you may attract. The one is the order of the charlatan, who trusts to factitious allurements for attracting the public, in the hope that he may cure some; the other, the order of the true physician, who trusts to the fact of his curing some as the means of attracting others. Wherever the Church is the means of making one shopman turn from his sins, and exhibit to his comrades a picture of holy living, in all probability she will soon have others from that shop at her altars. Whenever she brings one factory-girl to sit, like Mary, at the feet of Jesus, very probably other Marys will in a little while be with her. In every situation new converts are the most powerful attraction that ever acts on those who are still in the world. There seems a peculiar spiritual power connected with the first love, and an impressiveness in the words, of new converts, enforced by the manifest change in them, which nothing else can exert. That house of God which becomes noted in a neighbourhood as a place in which many sinners have been 'transformed by the renewing of their minds,' will, by a certain instinct of our redeemed humanity, soon become a centre of attraction, not only to those who, with scarcely any light, are groping after the truth, but even to many who are still hardily going on in sin. The greatest fame of Christianity is the fame of the cures she works, her greatest glory the glory of the saints she trains, her own unshared renown the renown of sinners renewed in the image of God; and wherever works of this kind are noised abroad in any community, there will the preacher not want hearers, there will the sower not be without a field."

Thomas Cook's early course as a lay evangelist, and indeed his whole career, is a striking illustration of the truth of these strong words of Mr. Arthur, for inserting which, notwithstanding that they have been before the reading world for well-nigh forty years, the writer offers no apology. He recently met a local preacher of many years' connection with Wesleyan Methodism, who, although a man who occasionally buys a book, and often reads one, had not only never seen the *Tongue of Fire*, but had not so much as heard that there was a William Arthur in our ministry. To such Methodists —and there are more than one—the above words will be as fresh as the morning newspaper; while others who are familiar with them will be glad to see them in this setting, and to find them amply vindicated in the story which the writer is narrating.

During this Low Moor mission the singing-band was made good use of. On one occasion, when the band was holding a half-hour's service in the streets, and many converts were testifying to the great change which Christ had wrought in them, the Evangelist pushed a man into the ring who was unknown to him, and supposed by him to be saved. It soon transpired, however, that Mr. Cook had mistaken his man; for when this poor fellow found himself in the middle of the ring, with hundreds of eyes fixed on him, he realised his position, and gave an unexpected turn to the proceedings by saying, " Friends, I ain't saved, but I mean to be to-night: God help me." The reader will not be surprised to learn that he who was put " into the pool " in this strange way was that night " made whole " by the Son of God.

The late Rev. Josiah Pearson was travelling in Bradford in the days of which this chapter treats, and at the Conference of 1882 he referred, in the conversation on the state of the Work of God, to some of the

E

events chronicled herein. Mr. Pearson stated that in his own Circuit (Manningham), and particularly in the White Abbey Chapel, a glorious work had been seen during the year. In one fortnight, he went on to say, upwards of six hundred persons gave in their names for the service of Christ, and the scenes he had witnessed would never be forgotten by him. After a hard day's work in the mills, the people went to chapel by hundreds, eighteen hundred to two thousand being present on the week-evening, and as many as a hundred inquirers had been pleading for mercy on the same night. The difficulty had been to get the services closed; many would fain have stayed all night to seek the Lord.

After describing the work in the Sunday school,—where, Mr. Pearson characteristically said, "the educational processes had to be stopped," with the result that an entire class of young men, which had been the cause of much trouble, were converted,—he proceeded to say that the class-meetings had since been well attended, the prayer-meetings were crowded, singing-bands were working the streets, and the work which the Salvation Army had set itself to do was being done in Bradford by the Methodists. He concluded by acknowledging the goodness of God in sending so rich a blessing to his Circuit, and said he prayed that similar visitations might be given to all parts of the Connexion.

Mr. Pearson has now been "with Christ" for some years. Whether or not he has finished some of those sermons,—portions of which he preached here, promising to complete them in heaven,—the writer cannot say. But there is much reason to believe that, however this may be, he has now met among the redeemed some who will ever be reckoned as part of the fruits of these mission services.

The Rev. Joseph Nettleton, who succeeded Mr. Pearson in the Manningham Circuit in 1885, writes :—

"On my appointment to the Circuit, I was greatly impressed with the abiding fruit of a mission that had been held there by the Rev Thomas Cook some years before. I found whole classes of young people who had been brought to Christ during that mission, and who had been growing in grace from the time of their conversion. They were earnest Christian workers, and were ever ready to support me in all kinds of aggressive evangelism, indoors or out of doors. They gathered other young people into the church, and conducted cottage services and open-air services. They woke up some of the older members, who were half asleep, and they kept them awake by getting them to work with them. I found these young people a great help to me in the Circuit, and several of them became local preachers and evangelists."

From the District Home Mission Sub-Committee's report, presented to the Halifax and Bradford District Committee, we learn that " Mr. Cook's labours were remarkably owned of God. The Churches were quickened, believers were sanctified, and many sinners were converted to God. During the first six months it was found, on careful inquiry, that 2000 persons above fifteen years of age, and a large number of younger people, had been helped in the inquiry-rooms; and, taking the whole of the first year, it is quite within the mark to say that 3000 persons professed to find peace with God. Of these, over 1000 adults were reported by the superintendent ministers of their respective Circuits as having begun to meet in class. Three hundred joined junior Society classes, and large numbers became connected with other Churches."

The report goes on to say, that in the second year Mr. Edward Davidson was engaged as Mr. Cook's colleague in the District work, and that then " a season of almost uninterrupted prosperity occurred. Thirty-one missions were held. Considerably more than 3000 inquirers were reported, in addition to a large number of children. About 2000 began to meet in class, and 800 joined other Churches." The reports speak of signal displays of saving and sanctifying power,—the entire consecration of believers being amongst the most important results.

CHAPTER V

CONNEXIONAL EVANGELIST.

MR. COOK'S success as a lay evangelist attracted much attention, as was natural, and tidings of it reached the ears of the late Rev. Alexander Macaulay, who was always on the alert for such news, and who had something to do with shaping Mr. Cook's course, as indeed he also had in introducing him to the Halifax and Bradford District Home Mission Sub-Committee. Mr. Cook became a candidate for the Wesleyan Methodist ministry the second time in 1881, and was then accepted, his work as a lay evangelist having proved that, whether he is entrusted with two talents or with five, God has assuredly called him to preach the gospel of His Son.

It is idle to blame "the July Committee" for declining to recommend Thomas Cook when he first offered for our ministry. Whatever *they* thought "against" him, "God meant it unto good, to bring to pass, as it is this day, to save much people alive." Had he been accepted then, it is certain that he would have been sent to the Theological Institution; for he was young, and he had not had the opportunity of proving that he was one of those God-given evangelists who are called to do special work, and who must not therefore be treated as others who are intended to occupy ordinary positions. Mr. Cook's own impression is, that "this thing was of God." Had he gone to the Institution, the probability is that, considering his extreme youth, his ministry would have assumed another form. Not that a college course is to be lightly esteemed; much less is it to be regarded as likely to destroy that earnest evangelistic spirit which our evangelist has so conspicuously displayed. Were the writer to imply this, he would bring down upon himself the ire of the more learned of his brethren, and involve himself in much trouble. Happily for himself, however, he is under no temptation to make any such observation. He remembers with satisfaction that some of the foremost evangelists of present-day Methodism have had the advantage of a college course, and have shown that their studies have made them more "meet for the Master's use" than they would otherwise have been. The Revs. J. H. Hopkins, Edward Smith, S. F. Collier, S. Chadwick, Edward Davidson, Thomas Waugh, Peter Thompson, and Hugh Price Hughes are all "Institution" men, and they have all well repaid Methodism for the expense and labour bestowed on their ministerial training.

In former years an opinion prevailed that culture and soul-saving fervour are incompatible, and it is possible that a lurking suspicion to that effect still lingers in the minds of some devout people; although it is surprising that, in a Connexion founded by a Fellow of Lincoln College, Oxford, who was also one of the most fervid of all evangelists, such a delusion should ever have obtained credence. Too often evangelistic work has been relegated to earnest but uncultured men; and sometimes it has been noticed, that as men have increased in knowledge their passion for souls has diminished. If any students who have enjoyed exceptional educational advantages should do the writer the honour to read these pages, he would venture to plead with them to make it their ambition to prove that it is possible to combine the highest culture with the intensest evangelistic fervour, and thus "unite the pair so long disjoined."

In the year 1882, Mr. Cook was received by the Wesleyan Methodist Conference as a minister on trial, and he was immediately appointed to do the work he loves so much, and to which God has so unmistakeably called him. Some of his friends did not approve of this arrangement, for they desired that he should be sent to the Institution. Thus Mr. J. Thorpe Taylor, of Holmfirth, who, perhaps, was as responsible as any one else for Mr. Cook's introduction to the Halifax and Bradford District, wrote, immediately after the Conference, as follows: "I was rather disappointed you were not to go to the Institution, as I believe you would there have derived lasting benefit, and also have influenced for good your fellow-students. But I am told you may have the chance of going next year; and meanwhile I trust you will be as happy and as useful in your new sphere of labour as you have been in this District during the last two years. What a wonderful work God has wrought by you, and those associated with you, during that period! Well may our hearts be filled with gratitude and our lips with praise!"

It should be stated that prior to the Conference of 1882 the Rev. Alexander Macaulay, then the General

Secretary of the Home Mission Department, wrote as follows to Mr. Cook: "I should like you to come under my care during next year, and intend to ask that this course may be taken in your appointment. While you are favoured with evangelistic success, such as you record, I think that you should continue to go from place to place. The Lord has dealt tenderly and bountifully with you, and as long as you keep humble and prayerful, He will honour you." Accordingly, in the Minutes of Conference for 1882, under the head of "Home Missions," the following record stands: "Thomas Cook, who shall act under the direction of the Home Missionary Committee." In the month of November 1882 the Rev. Dr. Bowden wrote thus in the *Methodist Recorder*:—

"'Thomas Cook, who shall act under the direction of the Home Missionary Committee,'— such is the quiet and modest record on the 'Minutes' of a new and important departure in Methodism,—a departure carefully considered and adopted by the Conference of 1880, but delayed until the providence of God gave the right man to do the work of a Connexional Evangelist. Such a man has been given this year in Thomas Cook, and an important movement of aggressive work has been begun, which we hope will greatly extend. A little while ago we were in serious danger from tame, pretty preaching. Sermonettes were laid upon the Bible by some men, and read without apparent feeling, or any attempt at direct appeal. If an earnest spirit of evangelism gets abroad, such preaching will either be 'killed or cured.' This, in itself, would be a Connexional blessing of no little worth. It is bad enough to listen to a pretty little essay, when the man has made it during the week, and it is fitted in some sense to the people who hear it; but it is very much worse when the weak discourse was written ten years ago, and is far removed from the sympathies of both the reader and the hearer. If an aggressive spirit prevails, and men preach the Word to save souls from death, there will be no place found for the small, cold, travelling essay, or for the man who carries it about with him. District missionaries have been for some years at work, and a missionary for the Connexion is the healthy development of that kind of service. The Methodist preachers were originally a band of evangelists moving to and fro, and waking up the parishes of the land. John Wesley gave them this rule, 'You have nothing to do but to save souls.' He intended them to be an auxiliary force to the parochial clergy. . Districts, Circuits, and preachers can become dormant and stagnant as surely as clergy and parishes. The preachers and class-leaders can keep the round of their classes and pulpits with conscientious regularity, and yet be half-asleep. The evangelist may be wanted to-day for the Circuit, as surely as a hundred and twenty years ago the Methodist preacher was needed for the parish. Both Circuits and preachers will be healthier, brighter, and more useful for a break in their routine, and for the presence of the man who has 'nothing to do but to save souls.' The spirit of aggression on the ungodliness and sin around us must be maintained in its vigour, or very soon the Church will not be able to hold its own. This Connexional evangelism is not only the expression of an aggressive spirit, but it will awaken and foster that spirit, and will thus increase not only the members in Society, but also the general vigour and strength of the Society, and thus prevent the 'scattering' which is inevitable, unless we continue to 'gather.' Methodism has had a time of chapel building and financial enterprise; we want now a time of chapel filling and good spiritual work, a revival in every Society."

The appointment of Mr. Cook as Connexional Evangelist was quickly followed by that of the Rev. Thomas Waugh, whose labours have also been remarkably blessed; and by that of the Rev. Edward Davidson, to whom reference has already been made in these pages more than once. The value of the services of these beloved brethren may be in some measure estimated by the large number of applications which are continually received for their help, that number never having been larger than it was this year.

To defend the appointment of Mr. Cook as our first Connexional Evangelist would be to admit that the arrangement has need of some defence, whereas we contend that God Himself has so manifestly sanctioned the appointment, that it requires no justification from the writer, or from any one else.

But it may be useful to add a few lines with the purpose of pointing out the relation that exists between the travelling evangelist and the settled pastor.

The Rev. Dr. Rigg, in the charge which he delivered to the newly-ordained ministers at the Birmingham Conference in the year 1879, observed, "In the apostolic age the office of evangelist would appear to have been one of wide scope, and allowing great latitude and variety of employment in the work of Christ. A great Church, like the united Church of the apostolic age, could not be complete without its corps of evangelists. Evangelists are necessary to complete our ministerial provision and equipment, acting now as home missionary ministers and district missionaries." Probably few of those who have reflected upon the subject will be disposed to differ from Dr. Rigg.

If all Circuit ministers had such success in the conversion of men as Robert Young, S. Romilly Hall, Thomas Vasey, and Thomas Nightingale, it might not then be necessary to set apart evangelists for this particular service. It has been truly said that if St. Peter was the apostle of the circumcision, and St. Paul of the uncircumcision, St. John was the apostle of the Church. Well has St. John been called "the divine," for his writings justify the pre-eminence which the title gives him, and they are naturally a favourite portion of Holy Scripture with all who conduct conventions for deepening the spiritual life of God's people. Possibly, however, St. John could not have given the evangelistic addresses which St. Peter and St. Paul gave, for it should seem that the apostles did not all receive the same spiritual gifts. A diversity of gifts characterises the ministry of the modern Church, if we may be permitted to say so, without it being supposed that we intend to encourage young ministers to believe that they are not called of God, "to open the eyes" of the unsaved, "and to turn them from darkness to light, and from the power of Satan unto God, that they may receive the forgiveness of sins." No Methodist preacher, at all events, should allow himself to fall into this delusion. At his ordination each Wesleyan minister receives a document which contains Mr. Wesley's "Twelve Rules of a Helper." To those rules are added these weighty words:—"Observe: It is not your business to preach so many times, and to take care merely of this or that Society, but to save as many souls as you can; to bring as many sinners as you possibly can to repentance, and with all your power to build them up in that holiness without which they cannot see the Lord." Wesleyan ministers are further reminded year by year that "every Methodist preacher is to consider himself as called to be in point of enterprise, zeal, and diligence a home missionary, and to enlarge as well as keep the Circuit to which he is appointed."

And, be it remembered, no Methodist preacher can claim to be recognised by his brethren as a fellow-labourer, if he does not continue to consent to these injunctions, and prayerfully endeavour, as God may help him, to fulfil them.

Nevertheless, it is to be feared that, notwithstanding such solemn admonitions, some modern Wesleyan ministers are in danger of neglecting the work of soul-saving, and leaving it to mission preachers and others. Possibly this circumstance may have given rise to the phrase, "The Forward Movement," which the writer himself never has adopted, and which he does not value, because it suggests that the Wesleyan ministry is divided. "The Forward Movement" cannot involve more than "The Twelve Rules of a Helper," and "The Liverpool Minutes" involve, and if any Wesleyan minister does *not* belong to a movement which is only the embodiment of the principles enjoined in those documents, he will do well to reconsider to what his ordination vows have committed him. The Rev. Hugh Price Hughes, M.A., who never carries the judgment of his brethren with him more entirely than when he is dealing with the subject of aggressive Christianity, and who is the chief exponent of the views of "The Forward Movement" party, if such party there be, published the following stirring remarks immediately after the close of the Nottingham Conference, in an article entitled, "Are our Ministers Ready?" Mr. Hughes writes:—

"A great and terrible delusion has taken possession of some of our ministers. We have heard men of high character and inflential positions say that they 'are called to edify the Church, and not to convert sinners.' They seem to imagine that the direct work of bringing sinners to Christ must be left to such evangelists as Mr. Thomas Cook and the agents of the great town missions. It is an indisputable fact that some of our ministers no longer expect immediate and visible results to their ministry. At one time Methodist preachers looked for converts, not only at the Sunday-evening service, but at the Sunday-morning service, at love-feasts and sacraments, and weekday services, and class-meetings. They assumed that the soul converting power would accompany them always and everywhere. Of course, they did not all expect to be instrumental in the salvation of sinners in the same way Some were so greatly blessed of God that sinners were converted under the Word, while the scriptural way of salvation was being expounded. Others reaped their harvest in pastoral visitation following up the impressions of the Lord's day. But in one way or other every Methodist preacher is expected to be a soul-winner. There are many reasons why that old expectation of unmistakeable conversions has passed into the background. What is needed above everything else is to revive it. The majority of the people of England are still outside all the Churches. The unsaved mass of grown-up men and women is immensely bigger to-day than it was when John Wesley mounted his horse and began his great evangel. Methodism cannot live without revivals and conversions. Mere Biblical expositions and pastoral education can never take the place of conspicuous, dramatic, glorious, personal conversions. By all means let everything else be done, but the supreme necessity is the proclamation of the gospel, with such faith and such fervour that the power of God may come down on the men and women who hear it, and deliver them from the slavery of sin."

If this is the policy of "The Forward Movement," who dare oppose it? But is not this the view which we *all* take of the situation? And yet, it must be admitted, there is need for the warning and rebuke and exhortation which Mr. Hughes' strong words convey. Let us listen to the Rev. John M'Neill, who, in a sermon on "The angels hastened Lot," says: "Even the warmest of us, are we as warm as we should be, as warm as we might be? Are we not a little afraid of earnestness? Hasn't it become a little unfashionable to plead with people? The angels were not ashamed to be in earnest. Hear it, hear it, hear it, ye superfines! The angels were not ashamed of being in dead earnest. Hear it, divinity students, coming preachers, the angels were not ashamed to be anxious and urgent, and to lay hold of people with their hands. I am afraid we, their successors, are losing ourselves. A large amount of present-day preaching will never serve the need. It is too dainty, it is too mighty fine altogether. The devil can stand it beautifully. He doesn't care how much of it goes on; it hurries up nobody."

God forbid that I should write one word that would weaken the force of these rebukes, for I am persuaded that if Methodism is " to reform the nation," and to " spread scriptural holiness over the land," the Methodist preachers, itinerant and lay, must as a body be baptized with this evangelistic spirit, and must not relegate to Connexional Evangelists or to the younger ministers the work of saving souls.

Nevertheless, it cannot be denied that it pleases God to confer on some ministers *extraordinary* evangelistic power. Speaking in his *Lectures on Preaching* of this gift, that great preacher, Dr. Dale, observes: " In some cases this power seems to have come to a man at the very beginning of his own religious life; in others, after many years of patient and earnest Christian work, which had achieved no extraordinary success; in some cases it has rested upon a man for a time and then been withdrawn." Dr. Dale adds a few words which I will subjoin, because they justify the appointment of Mr. Cook to the position of Connexional Evangelist, which appointment was made a few years after the publication of Dr. Dale's *Lectures*. " The man on whom extraordinary evangelistic power is conferred must, as a rule, separate himself from the ordinary duties of the pastorate. He is appointed to other work, and must not decline it. His position is one of exceptional honour, and also of exceptional peril. He should be strengthened and sustained by the constant intercessions of the Church." Animated by such sentiments as these, the Wesleyan Conference of 1882, as we have seen, set Mr. Cook apart for this particular service, and during the years that have intervened since then he has given himself wholly to the work, with results that call for devout thanksgiving from all who are interested in the evangelisation of this country.

Some of our readers will remember that years ago the Wesleyan Methodist Conference was embarrassed by the labours of the Rev. James Caughey in British Methodism. Mr. Caughey was undoubtedly a man of God, and his ministry here was much blessed. But he was not a member of the English Conference, nor was he amenable to our ecclesiastical courts. It was therefore not surprising that it was impossible for Mr. Caughey to fill our pulpits without throwing out of gear our ecclesiastical machinery sooner or later.

By appointing Mr. Cook to the office of Connexional Evangelist, the Conference secured the advantage of his God-given evangelistic power, and at the same time secured itself against the occurrence of irregularities, Mr. Cook being a member of its own body, and responsible to his brethren for his teaching and methods and conduct.

As a matter of fact, the arrangement has worked perfectly. The Evangelist has been allowed the fullest liberty. The largest chapels in the Connexion have been placed at his disposal, and he has had all the advantages of one of the most complete ecclesiastical organisations in the world; while, on the other hand, Methodism has reaped a precious harvest from his labours.

The influence of the appointment was felt in America. The *New York Christian Advocate* directed attention to it, and remarked that it was worthy of the serious consideration of the Methodist Episcopal Church. That journal pointed out that American Methodism had suffered from the employment of irregular and uncertain evangelists, and it declared that if the Church which it represented were to follow the example of the English Conference, and to appoint not one, but two or three, of its own ministers to this work, the results would in all probability be such as none but God Himself could measure.

Mr. Cook's first mission as the Connexional Evangelist was held, soon after the Conference of 1882, in the city of Bristol. The mission lasted for three weeks, during which time upwards of six hundred adults entered the inquiry-rooms. Services were held occasionally at one o'clock in the afternoon, and were, according to the testimony of Dr. Bowden, who was then stationed in Bristol, more largely attended than the ordinary Sunday-evening services, whilst at the services which were held later in the day all the seats were occupied. It would, of course, be impossible to follow Mr. Cook through every mission which he has held during the last nine years, nor is it necessary to attempt to do this. Some of his most successful missions have been conducted at Walsall, Sheffield, West Bromwich, Oldham, Pendleton, Leeds, Cardiff, Portsmouth, Exeter, Dublin, and in various Circuits in

F

Cornwall. During his first year of Connexional work he saw a gracious revival in the Centenary Chapel, Boston. Over five hundred persons sought salvation, most of whom must have found what they sought, for at a meeting held at the close of the mission to recognise the converts, and welcome them into the Church, three hundred of them were present and received from their pastors "notes on trial." The effects of the mission was seen three months later, when the stewards reported to the Circuit Quarterly Meeting a good increase of income, and the Superintendent reported an increase on the quarter of two hundred and twenty-two members, with one hundred and sixty-seven on trial, and eighty-nine in junior classes.

In no part of the country is Methodism more influential or more prosperous than in Cardiff, where we have the advantage of much splendid chapel property, and the still greater advantage of the support of many able and godly men who have understanding of the times, and know what Israel ought to do. In 1883, Mr. Cook held a mission in the fine Roath Road Wesleyan Chapel. Mr. Lewis Williams, J.P., reports that the first Lord's day of the mission was a memorable day in the history of the Sunday school. The first to go into the inquiry-room that afternoon was the ringleader of a troublesome class of boys whose ages ranged from sixteen to twenty. Then many more young people followed. At the first Sunday-evening service twenty-five adults sought the Lord. On the second Sunday afternoon a men's meeting was held, attended by a thousand men, and that day there were one hundred inquirers. Mr. Lewis Williams writes: "During the singing of the first hymn a young man literally rushed into the inquiry-room. At night two stalwart men got up during the singing of the second hymn, one of them groaning aloud, 'Lord, help; Lord, save me!' His distress was beyond description. Nineteen times he had been imprisoned. The case bears unmistakeable proof of genuineness. He is now as red-hot in the Lord's service as he was formerly in the devil's. One of the remarkable features of this revival is, that whilst it reached the wealthy, it also reached the veriest outcasts, one of whom said, 'Last Sunday found me playing at pitch and toss.' Another said, 'I was then yielding to swearing and dissipation of the worst kind.' At the close of the mission Mr. Cook held a meeting for the converts, five hundred of them being present, and suitably addressed them. The number of stalwart men amongst the converts, and of persons of middle age, was very striking. Nearly all the class of boys to which reference has been made were among those who that evening professed to have found peace with God, and many who at first ridiculed the mission were in the happy throng. The number of cases of parties who have made restitution to present and former employers, indicates the depth of this work of God. The Holiness-meetings were well attended, and most edifying. Over five hundred adults and one hundred and twenty children entered the inquiry-rooms. Many of these will join other Churches, but we have formed seven new classes, and our people are busy gathering the fruit into our spiritual barns. The mission has stirred the whole town, and is now being followed up by missions in other parts of the Circuit."

In no town have Mr. Cook's labours been more

abundantly owned of God than in Sheffield. The Rev. W. Middleton reports that the names of seven hundred inquirers were taken during the first ten days; while before the mission closed in Carver Street Chapel the names of nine hundred were taken in that place alone, forty-five *men* coming out as penitents at the men's service, and one hundred and forty-six adults doing the same at the closing Sunday-evening service. Mr. Middleton states that two hundred of the converts promised to join the Carver Street Society, and fifty the junior classes, while fifty belonged to other Methodist churches; one hundred to various denominations, and one hundred had not been settled. Six months afterwards Mr. Middleton writes: " Our numbers and the interest in the work of God are very well sustained in this [Carver Street] Circuit. In June we reported an increase of one hundred and twenty-eight, and we have still three hundred and fifty-three members on trial. We shall have another increase in September. I do praise God that in these summer months we are all alive. The last twice at Carver Street I have had an open-air service, instead of the prayer-meeting in the chapel, followed by a prayer-meeting in the young men's room, and we have had penitents. I find encouragement in this, that during the year I have preached eleven times in Carver Street Chapel on Sunday evenings, and at every service have had conversions, from one to fourteen."

The Rev. W E. Codling reports, that amongst Mr. Cook's converts at that mission was a man who wrung his hands, saying, "If I had only been converted twenty years ago, there are some in hell who would not have gone there." Mr. Codling says an old man sat weeping on a form in the inquiry-room, his face showing that he was no stranger to pugilistic encounters. "My friend," said the minister to him, "I see you know you are a sinner." "I am that," said the old man: "and a bigger sinner than anybody in this place. Many a time on a Sunday morning I have gone out to fight for money. And now, when I am an old man, and suffering for my sins, here I run to the Lord, like a big coward. But I'll fight for Jesus now." A mother who, two years before, had been bereaved of a child, and who had been seeking the Saviour ever since, pointed upwards and said, "There she is, and now I know I am going to her." As Mr. Cook was walking to the chapel one evening, an aged man, evidently full of gratitude, seized him by the arm, saying, "Ay, mon, do you know, I've got saved at Carver Street. I've served the devil seventy years and three weeks." Mr. Codling adds, that one evening a boy sent a request for prayer to be offered for the conversion of his grandfather, grandmother, and brother, all of whom were consciously saved before the mission closed.

Such are a few of the many interesting and pathetic incidents that occurred during this blessed mission in Sheffield. It should be added, that simultaneous services were conducted by other evangelists in several Wesleyan chapels in Sheffield whilst the Carver Street mission was going on, and that great good was accomplished by this united effort, which made a deep and permanent impression upon the town. It was my privilege to take a humble part in the closing services of this united mission, and I can bear testimony to the wide-spread interest which it evoked. The local press paid much attention to the mission, and inserted "leaders" on the subject, and thus brought the movement before the whole town. Something is gained when the newspaper press is made an arm of the service. When the mission preacher is a man of God, the notice thus given him should not puff him up; while the mention of these things in the secular press brings the question of personal salvation before many who seldom or never attend the house of God. It is not, perhaps, the least praise of Thomas Cook, that he has compelled newspaper writers in many parts of the country to report the doings of one whose only "business here below" is "to cry, Behold, behold, the Lamb!"

On the day following the close of the united mission in Sheffield, the local newspapers, which had, as we have seen, paid much attention to the mission, informed their readers that Mr. Samuel Osborn had, on the previous evening, sent out cheques to the value of £23,000 to former creditors of his, with whom many years before he had compounded, and whose moral, but not legal, claims he had resolved to discharge, and had accordingly fully met. It is not meant to imply that this honourable conduct on the part of the late Samuel Osborn—who died in 1891, being at the time Mayor of Sheffield—was due in any measure to the events now being reviewed, because, as a matter of fact, he had cherished the purpose to do it for some years. It will, however, be seen that this instance of fine commercial integrity—coming as it did in the wake of a great evangelistic movement, which had arrested the attention of the whole town—must have deeply impressed that great industrial community, and caused

Wesleyan-Methodism to have " favour with all the people."

" Go, sell the oil, and pay thy debt," said the prophet to the widow; and when debts are paid by businessmen for which they are not legally liable, more is done to glorify God by " good works " than would be done by the erection of a chapel or the building of an orphanage with the money. Seeing that Christianity has so often been discredited by conduct the reverse of the late Mr. Osborn's, we are the more pleased to notice his action in this matter, where " integrity and uprightness " preserved him.

The Tiviot Dale Chapel, Stockport, is as noble a structure as can be found in Methodism, and in 1884 it was the scene of a gracious visitation, of which the Rev. J. D. Stevens writes: " Never since Tiviot Dale Chapel was built have such scenes been witnessed in it as were seen during Mr. Cook's mission. The congregations steadily increased as the mission proceeded. During the first week the chapel, large as it is, was for the most part well filled. But from the second Sunday the place was all too small; and from some of the services hundreds had to go away, there being no room for them. On the evening of the second Sunday the Rev. J. Nattrass held an overflow service in the school-room. At the close of the mission it was found that the names of seven hundred and forty adults and four hundred children had been taken in the inquiry-rooms. About a third appear to belong to other Churches. The special meetings for women, and for children, and for the promotion of holiness, were greatly blessed. But perhaps the most extraordinary of all the meetings were those for men only, held in the afternoons of the second and third Sundays. To see the large chapel filled in every part with men, and especially to see the large number that went into the inquiry-room, was a sight never to be forgotten. The work in the inquiry-rooms was most interesting— almost every variety of case and character presented itself there. Members of our classes, children of our people, life-long hearers of the Word, and others who had not heard the Word for years, knelt side by side. Here was a little girl, who, having sought and found the Saviour, came the next night to pray for her mother. Here was a woman who had not said the Lord's Prayer for six years because she would not forgive her brother; and not far off was the keeper of a notorious house. In addition to all the rest, and as important as all the rest, the mission has resulted in a quickened Church. No collection was made; but the free-will offerings of the people, placed in boxes at the doors, provided more than enough to cover the expenses."

From Stockport, Mr. Cook went to West Bromwich, where he held a much-blessed mission in the spacious Wesleyan Chapel. If any reader thinks it a light matter to get this large chapel full on a week-evening for an evangelistic service, let him apply for the use of it for that purpose, and test his opinion in a practical way.

The Rev. J. P Keeley reported as follows: "The noble and spacious edifice was filled to overflowing at every evening service, and in the afternoons the congregations were also very large. The addresses then given on holiness were much appreciated. The men's meeting was a sight never to be forgotten. Sixteen hundred men were present, and many of the unsaved yielded themselves to Christ. The young people of the school and belonging to our families received much attention from Mr. Cook, and many of them were much blessed. All sorts and conditions of people have attended the services, some coming from distant places. The revival is spreading throughout the Circuit; and other Circuits and other Churches have felt the good effects of the work, which is manifestly of the Lord. We report with great joy, that one thousand and forty-eight persons have professed to find peace with God during the mission. Of this number, five hundred and twenty-eight have signified their intention to join our own Society. About three hundred belong to other Churches, and their names and addresses have been forwarded to their respective pastors. To God be all the glory! The expenses of the mission were about £50, and were more than met by the contributions, which were placed in boxes at the doors, no collection being made in the chapel. We sent £10 to the Home Mission Fund as a thank-offering for Mr. Cook's services."

The only comments that our space will permit are these: the student of the problem of evangelisation will not fail to notice that a large proportion of the converts of each mission are said to belong to other Churches. This was so in West Bromwich, where, when all the facts were known, it was found that one in three of the converts were connected with some other Church, and were not lawful prey for our class-leaders, who are taught to hate sheep-stealing as much as some others—who suppose that to save souls from "schism" is equal to saving them from sin—are taught to love that practice. It must also be borne in mind that it is not possible to trace *every* convert, how well soever the pastor may know his flock. Some converts arrive in safety "where all the ship's company meet" before they have had time to identify themselves with any particular Church; and others, for various reasons, live and die outside the visible fold of Christ, although, according to the sound theological teaching of the "bairn's hymn," because they loved the Lord, when they died they went to heaven. The first time St. Paul went to Italy he "found brethren" at Puteoli, somewhat to his surprise, as we gather from the tenor of the narrative, for, so far as is known, no formal mission had been sent thither; and whose converts these "brethren" were, no man knows. President Lincoln was some one's convert, but he held aloof from church membership; so was also Samuel Livesey, of temperance fame, who did likewise. "The day will declare" the number of those who, being "ordained to eternal life, believed." "Other sheep I have which are not of this flock," said our Lord. May He not have sheep which are not of any flock of which we have knowledge? "Nevertheless the foundation of God standeth sure, having this seal, *The Lord* knoweth them that are His."

Walsall is a neighbouring town to West Bromwich, and here also Mr. Cook saw the arm of the Lord revealed in a most extraordinary manner. The late Rev. Dr. James writes: "About fifty persons found peace with God on the first day, and this proved to be the commencement of a work which in some of its features I have never seen equalled. The congregations rapidly increased, and great numbers were converted—at least four hundred during the first week. On the second Sunday afternoon a service for men only was held. It was a wonderful and almost awful sight—fifteen hundred men at least gathered together to hear words whereby they might be saved, and to wait for the kingdom of God. That day about a hundred were added to the number of the saved, and the next day, and the following, a hundred and forty more. The climax of interest and triumph was, however, reached on the succeeding day. In the afternoon the chapel was filled with women. At night an enormous congregation of nearly three thousand persons was gathered together, and at the close of the day it was found that nearly two hundred and twenty persons had entered the inquiry-room, nearly all of whom had professed to find peace with God. On Thursday, the last day of the mission, a hundred more were added to the number. The attention of the town was arrested, and a manifest feeling of awe and wonder prevailed. The local papers published appreciative articles on the mission. On the last evening, when no doubt the congregation numbered nearly three thousand, hundreds were turned away for want of room. The converts numbered nine hundred." Dr. James then gives a statement which shows to what Churches the converts had elected to go, and concludes his report thus: "I can only adore the mercy which permits an old campaigner, at the end of nearly fifty years' service, to witness the greatest spiritual triumph he has ever been privileged to see." Two months later Dr James wrote: "The converts appear to hold on well. We had three hundred and seventy-three members on trial in this Circuit *alone* [at the quarterly meeting], and there are numbers in other Circuits and Churches in the neighbourhood."

Another large mission was held about this time at Pendleton, in the Irwell Street Circuit, Manchester. The writer himself was present at one of the services of this mission, and could therefore report his own impressions. But let the late Rev. George Walker, being dead, yet speak of what he saw at that time. Mr. Walker was then the Superintendent of the Circuit, and his report was as follows: "During the first week the congregations increased each evening, and four hundred persons above fourteen years of age professed decision. The second Sunday commenced with a remarkable service at seven A.M. About six hundred were present, including nearly all who had found Christ during the previous week, and others who had received answers to prayer in the salvation of friends. After offering praise to God, the congregation went out and formed a ring in front of the chapel, where several hymns were sung. They then formed a procession, in which educated young ladies and sober men of business, to their own astonishment, felt constrained to walk, and went singing through the back streets. The service for men only, in the afternoon, was most impressive. About fifteen hundred men were present, nearly fifty of whom decided for Christ, some of the cases of conversion being remarkable. In the evening the chapel was crowded, and one hundred and twenty-six entered the inquiry-rooms. Wednesday was a day never to be forgotten. At three P.M. the chapel was filled with women, and about a hundred yielded to Christ. In the evening the crowd was almost awful; the interior of the spacious building presented the sight of one mass of living beings all bowed down under the presence of God. Three hundred persons professed to find peace with God. On the last day of the mission about seven hundred of the converts occupied the body of the chapel, while the galleries were crowded with others, and hundreds were unable to obtain admission. Mr. Cook gave an impressive address to the newly converted, and then made a final appeal to the unsaved, and one hundred and thirty responded, and entered the inquiry-rooms. The meetings for the promotion of holiness were seasons of grace and sweet delight. The total number of converts exceeded eleven hundred, of whom more than half belonged to other places of worship. Probably a hundred were already attending class. At the communion service about one half of the five hundred communicants stood up to confess that it was their first communion. The people are crowding the classes; numbers who did not go into the inquiry-rooms are joining the Church. The band-meetings and prayer-meetings are attended by hundreds."

The mission which Mr. Cook held during this period at Oldham was as extraordinary for results as any of the missions here described. The writer was then stationed in Manchester, and had himself opportunities for forming a judgment upon the work. But let the Rev. William Potts, who was on the ground, give evidence. After describing the first week, Mr. Potts writes: "The second Sunday was a day never to be forgotten. In the afternoon the chapel was crowded with men, fifteen hundred being present, and a good number yielded to the powerful appeals of the Mission preacher. At the evening service hundreds were unable to get into the chapel. The names of about seven hundred and fifty inquirers were taken, of whom one hundred and thirty belong to other Churches. The sons and daughters of some of our best families, long prayed for, have been brought to God. The power of God was overwhelming in the meetings for the promotion of holiness. The expenses were large, but were more than met by free-will offerings. A balance of £20 left over will be sent to the Home Mission Fund as a thankoffering."

Mr. Potts' reference to "the sons and daughters of our best families" suggests an observation with which the patient reader must be troubled. We have already seen, and we shall yet see in a much larger measure, that it has been the great joy of Mr. Cook to lead many young people to Christ. Mr. Cook is still a young evangelist,—and "to be young is very heaven,"—and his youth may have attracted the young to him. But what minister is there who does not earnestly covet the power to influence for good the children of the members of his flock? I do not see what reason we have to expect that we shall succeed in keeping to Methodism the sons and daughters of our more prosperous people unless we succeed in bringing them to Christ. If Methodist preaching is what it ought to be, it will repel from Methodism these young people unless it leads them to Christ. Such preaching is too searching to be endured passively; and hence it is not surprising that many educated young men and young women, who have not yielded to Christ, have left the Church of their fathers, and, under the pretence of seeking something more cultured, either in preaching or in ritual, have betaken themselves to "quiet resting-places." Nor can we hope to grapple these young people to Methodism with literary societies and choral societies, however innocent or even useful such organisations may be. "The sovereign'st thing on earth" for this ailment, *i.e.* discontentedness with the Church of one's fathers, is sound conversion to God, followed by a deep and an intelligent interest in the work of God. There are—God be praised—some of the children of our best families, old Leysians and others, so engrossed in Methodist work, and so happy in it, that they are insensible to the charms of high-class music and a gorgeous ritual; neither do they wish to forsake their own people and their fathers' people for the sake of what is politely called "society." They are as contented as was the Shunammite, who cared not to be spoken for even to the king; but their contentment is due to this, they have found that kingdom which is like treasure hid in a field. Let us seek first for the children of Methodism—and especially for our own children—"the kingdom of God and His righteousness," for if they obtain this, there is much reason to believe that amongst the "all things" that will be added to them, will be a firm and an intelligent attachment to the Church to which they belong by birth.

Leaving the great industrial centres of the North, we may follow the course of our Evangelist to Portsmouth, in which large town he held a mission during the earlier part of this period. Portsmouth being a great military and naval centre, it is not surprising, although it is humiliating and painful, to hear that it is also the centre of much iniquity, the truth being that the forces of good and of evil are actively at work amongst that large population. Some of the most devoted Wesleyan-Methodists the writer has known during the last one-and-twenty years have been found in the Portsmouth Societies, and amongst those Societies there are now to be found some of the most precious fruits of Mr. Cook's ministry. As an instance of the power of prayer, it may be here stated that some time before Mr. Cook visited Portsmouth, and indeed before his existence was known to the authorities of the Circuits in the town, three or four praying men met together in an informal way to plead with God for the outpouring of His Spirit upon the congregations. It so happened that at that time peculiar difficulties had arisen in the Circuit to which they belonged,—difficulties which no human skill seemed able to surmount, and which greatly impeded the progress of the work of God. A few earnest men, who were and still are deeply interested in the Circuit, made prayer without ceasing unto God for the removal of these obstacles. An assurance was given them that God would take the matter into His own hands; and, as the writer was told only a few days before these pages were written, by one of these brethren who took the most active part in the proceedings, when as yet they did not know that there was such a man living as Thomas Cook, they were assured by God that ere long hundreds would be converted in their Circuit, and that all the hindrances to the prosperity of the work would be swept away by a mighty outpouring of the Spirit of God. It was done unto them according to their faith. The

Rev Richard Hardy writes: " The evening services were crowded. Pentecostal blessings resulted. Those who never entered God's house, as well as the unsaved who frequented it, were awakened and converted. Drunkards, wrestling with their foe as in a death struggle, gave up the drink, and on their knees sought the Saviour. The child of eight and the old man of seventy-seven were kneeling at the Cross near each other. To use the expression of a sailor of the Royal Navy, 'Hundreds wept their way to Calvary.' At the close of the mission the Wesleyan ministers of the town, with the members of the Circuit quarterly meeting and their wives, met to consider how the revival could be perpetuated and extended; and this gathering of about one hundred officials passed a resolution expressive of their devout gratitude to God for the conversions that had occurred, and for the deepening of the spiritual life of the Societies, and their earnest hope that the mission would prove to be the beginning of a continuous and extended revival of the work of God in the Circuits of the town. Amongst the converts was the keeper of a public-house, who, as soon as he was converted, proceeded to cut off his right hand by informing the owner of the tied house that he must be instantly released from his occupation, as his conscience would not now permit him to follow that trade. The owner demurred; but the convert was firm, and said that unless another man was put into the house forthwith, he should close the doors, as he could not carry on the business any longer. Within a week he and his wife were out of the pernicious trade, and were in the class-meeting, happy in the love of God, because, like Levi, who, when sitting at the receipt of custom, was called to follow Christ, left all, rose up, and followed Him, they had left all to be the disciples of the Lord Jesus Christ. Another convert was a man who had been much addicted to intemperance, and who was not rescued without much earnest and prayerful effort. After his conversion it transpired that he was in debt to the amount of eight pounds to a local publican, and thereupon one of the workers in the mission, who was not by any means known as a well-to-do man, discharged the whole liability, that the convert might not be exposed to the temptation which would arise if he visited the public-house merely for the sake of paying by instalments the debt he owed. " With *such* sacrifices God is well pleased."

These converts still retain the blessing they then found, and the reader will admit that revivals that bear such fruit as this are a continuation of the work that was done in Ephesus, when " many of them also which used curious arts brought their books together, and burned them before all men; and they counted the price of them, and found it fifty thousand pieces of silver. So mightily grew the Word of God, and prevailed."

Nor were the instances just cited exceptional occurrences. Many more might be given of a like kind. Were space less valuable, much might be said of restitution made by converts for wrong done to others years ago, and also of young ladies who laid aside the sin that did so easily beset them, and never wore new ball dresses which they had purchased before their conversion, in order that they might " run with patience the race set before " them. But we must stay our hand.

In February 1888, Mr. Cook visited Exeter, and here also he was permitted to gather "fruit unto life eternal." At the seven o'clock Sunday morning prayer-meeting four hundred were present, and three persons sought the Lord at that early hour. The Rev. W. Spilsbury took charge of the inquirers, and Mr. Cook led the congregation outside for the purpose of awakening the attention of the neighbourhood. The snow was lying on the ground, but the hearts of the people were warm, and mission hymns were sung, much to the surprise of the late risers, who could not understand the meaning of this unusual and, as many would doubtless think, unseasonable disturbance. During this mission at Exeter four hundred and forty-one adults professed to seek peace with God, as did also one hundred and thirty-two children. It was stated in the local newspaper that "the oldest worshipper in the chapel did not remember such a series of enthusiastic and God-blest services as were held during the fortnight." At the close of the mission the Rev. W Spilsbury presented Mr. Cook with a handsome copy of the *Analytical Concordance*, and about twenty other books, on behalf of the united Societies of the town.

This was an unusual circumstance, for Mr. Cook wisely discourages such manifestations of goodwill, because he wishes to "walk in wisdom toward them that are without." Like St. Paul, he does not "desire a gift." Nevertheless, like the same apostle, he has once and again been constrained to accept one, not being always able to check the generosity of converts who are eager to give their fathers in Christ, not only "Concordances," but to "pluck out [their] own eyes" and give them also, if that were "possible."

Mr. Cook's ministry has not been confined to Great Britain; in Ireland also he has gathered many sheaves. He held a mission in Dublin which was described in the press at the time by an independent witness as "more than a Methodist mission, inasmuch as it reached all classes and creeds, and awakened an interest (if nothing more) in spiritual matters amongst thousands who previously were quite careless." The services were crowded, many Roman Catholics being amongst the hearers; and the names of seven hundred inquirers were taken, all the Protestant Churches and the Roman Catholic Church being represented on the lists.

A writer, unknown to myself, in a report of the Dublin mission makes the following just observations:—

"Mr. Cook is one of the best evangelists of this generation. His sermons are not remarkable for eloquence, originality, or thoughtfulness. They are remarkable for plain, pointed, earnest appeals. The interest never flags, the great question of present decision for God is never lost sight of, and all through there is an unction from the Holy One. His management of a meeting is beyond praise. His ready tact, his power of command, his tender sympathy, give constant opportunities for wonder and delight. The principal cause of success is found in the afternoon meetings for holiness. Here Mr. Cook is seen at his best. His clear views, his telling illustrations, his powerful appeals at these meetings, can never be forgotten. A new life seems to be before Methodism in Dublin."

We shall have occasion in a subsequent chapter

to refer again to this Dublin mission, and will therefore proceed to notice one or two missions held elsewhere, before the space left at our disposal for this chapter is exhausted.

In March 1889, Mr. Cook visited Leeds, and held a mission in the historic Brunswick Chapel. During the course of the mission five hundred adults publicly sought salvation, and the people of God themselves were richly blessed at the holiness meetings and other services. The men's meeting was attended by nineteen hundred men, and was most impressive; while the women's meeting, held on a week-day afternoon, was attended by twelve hundred. The converts belonged to all classes, and included persons of refinement as well as aged people. Many young people were also included in the list of the saved. The widow of a local preacher sent a request for prayer for the conversion of her only son, a young man of five-and-twenty. Prayer was offered, and the same night he was in the inquiry-room. An elderly man, for whom several people had prayed for fifteen years, was brought to God. "Praise God," said one of the workers, "my mother, for whom I have prayed these seventeen years, has just gone into the inquiry-room." A youth, who had come out of gaol in the morning, came to the service in the evening. He had been well trained, but had gone astray. In the cell he had obtained God's forgiveness, and he went forward to tell of His goodness and mercy. In one of the services, five young ladies, all from the same place of business, were brought to decision.

A ministerial correspondent writes of this Brunswick Chapel mission: "One thing is clear: the old-fashioned truth, simply and earnestly preached in the old-fashioned Methodist way, has still a charm for the people, and is still blessed of God to the salvation of souls. We had eighteen services in ten days. Would eighteen lectures or concerts or entertainments in ten days have drawn such crowds and commanded such deep attention? In Mr. Cook's sermons there is no mere intellectual effect, no modern thought, but, instead, there is deep and earnest warning, close and powerful wrestling with the conscience and with the will, and solemn appeal. Some of his sermons were to me like an echo of those which I used to hear in my boyhood, and which have been, alas! too scarce in modern years. But it is under these sermons —occasionally almost terrible in their solemnity— that men and women are awakened, and led to decision for God. Oh, for more of such preaching, and for more of the divine power to accompany the Word!"

It has been the joy of Mr. Cook to lead many sinners to Christ in London also. Much might be written of successful missions held in Southwark, Willesden, and other parts of the metropolitan district, but we will omit further reference to these missions, and devote a few lines to the mission which Mr. Cook held in Hampstead in 1890. It might have been supposed that at Hampstead, if anywhere in the world, a mission would have been, if not barren, certainly not very fruitful. Methodism has not flourished at Hampstead, although it has not been without vigorous supporters in that charming suburb. It should seem that the soil is not congenial for the growth of Methodism, and we should be disposed to believe that this is so, and that this explains our want of success there, if it were not for two circumstances: one of these is the great success of the Rev. R. F. Horton, M.A., at Hampstead. Before Mr. Horton's advent it was thought that Congregationalism would never succeed in Hampstead, where the population is largely made up of artists and other professional men, and where the rents of the houses are exceedingly high. Yet no sooner was it noised abroad that there was *a man* in the pulpit of the Congregational Church at Hampstead, than the people crowded to hear his message.

The other circumstance is the mission which Mr. Cook held at Hampstead. Of this mission the Rev. T. E. Westerdale sent a report to the *Methodist Recorder*, which, though printed in small type, occupied a column and a half, and which, if it were reprinted here, would make all my writing appear tameness itself. I must be content to say that Mr. Westerdale declares that he shall never forget as long as he lives the scenes which he witnessed during that revival, where a hundred and seventy-eight souls were converted to God.

From the report of Mr. Cook's labours during his first year as Connexional Evangelist, we gather that in that period he saw three thousand seven hundred adults and nearly two thousand children seeking salvation in his services. The report for the second year gives us larger numbers still, for during the second year some of these large missions were held of which this chapter treats. The report for 1886-87 also lies before us, and shows that the work of that year was even more prosperous than ever, that it was, in truth, unprecedented in Mr. Cook's experience. In this year (1886-87) he visited places of which no mention has been made—Skipton, Birmingham, Bradford, Leek, Gainsborough, Leicester, Launceston, and Zetland being among the number.

The work has shown no abatement of fruit-bearing power since then. In a private letter which Mr. Cook addressed to me at the close of the winter season of 1891, he stated that "the missions of the year 1890-91 had been amongst the most successful that he has ever held." The places visited that year were not of such Connexional importance as some of those to which reference is here made, and perhaps the numerical results were not always as large, but the work of the year, as a whole, was equally successful, and calls for devout thanksgiving from all who wish to see the gospel spread throughout these islands.

Mr. Cook entered upon this work with some fear and trembling; for he was young, inexperienced, without much resource, and the position was one of much prominence, bringing him before the whole Connexion, and especially before the ministers with whom he had to work, and many of whom are always in his services. Never could he have faced these responsibilities had he not been assured that although, like the prophet Jeremiah, he was but "a child," his "sufficiency was of God." Mr. Cook has publicly said in the writer's hearing that when he first began his work, he had, as it were, but five loaves and two small fishes. This slender provision, however, he took to his Master, who blessed it, and made it go so far that he himself has been greatly astonished. In this respect his experience is like Bunyan's. During his prison days Bunyan was once expected to preach to his fellow-prisoners; but Bunyan felt himself empty, spiritless, and barren, and unable to speak five words of truth with life and evidence. Then there came a break in the clouds, and Bunyan saw something in the chapter of the Word of God which was before him. Bunyan carried his "meditations to the Lord Jesus for a blessing, which He did forthwith grant according to His grace; and helping me to set before my brethren, we did all eat and were well refreshed; and behold, also, that while I was in the distributing of it, it so increased in my hand, that of the fragments that we left, after we had well dined, I gathered up this basketful." "The basketful" left sufficed to make one of his prison books, his *Holy City*, published in 1665, and it still remains fresh and useful.

I have desired in this chapter to avoid the use of all sensational and extravagant terms, and have for the greater part given the testimonies of eye-witnesses of the scenes here described, chiefly, if not entirely, of brother ministers. If, however, the reader has detected any tendency on my part to magnify the work which Thomas Cook has been enabled to do, he must accept my assurance that the one wish of the Evangelist and of the writer is that the reader should be compelled to exclaim: "This is the Lord's doing, and it is marvellous in our eyes."

CHAPTER VI.

PRINCIPLES AND METHODS OF WORK.

THE late Field-Marshal Count von Moltke, who in 1870–71 conducted a successful war on behalf of his country with France, states, in the account of the war which has recently been published, that "everything in military history is judged by its results."

Mr. Cook has conducted a holy war in this country during the last ten years, and, judged by its results, we must admit that during this ten years' war the Evangelist has been as victorious in his "line of things" as the German Field-Marshal was in his particular sphere. This imperfect account of the evangelistic war is written, that it may do for the student of Christianity what the Field-Marshal's description of the Franco-German war is intended to do for the student of military science.

For, whatever may be thought of Mr. Cook's preaching, principles, and methods, no candid person who is familiar with the facts can for one moment deny that, "judged by its results," his ministry has been phenomenally successful. Vinet reminds us that "preaching is an action." If a sermon is not intended *to do something*, why should it be preached? If the sermon is merely listened to, however learned, eloquent, and beautiful it may be, it must be regarded as a failure. The most learned preacher living preaches to no purpose unless he has a purpose in preaching.

Mr. Cook has a purpose, and only one: it is to save himself and them that hear him. And because he has effected his purpose, and saved his hearers and himself hitherto, it may be worth while to study his principles and methods. A junior minister went to hear Mr. Cook preach on one occasion, and afterwards reported to a senior minister that there was not a great deal in the sermon he heard, for it was full of "Come, come, come." "But," said the elder to the younger, "*did* they come?" "They did," was the reply; "they streamed down the aisles, greatly to my surprise." "Then," said the senior man, "you ought to go again, and to keep on going, till you have learned to say 'Come' with like results." We have all heard sermons in our time—some of us, alas! have preached such sermons—that have been "full of Come, come, come," and yet those whom we have thus importuned have *not* come. If to tell men that they ought to repent and believe the gospel, and to entreat them with vehemence to come to Christ, were all that is necessary to produce results, who of us would be unsuccessful? If any man should think it sufficient to say, "We adjure you by Jesus whom Thomas Cook preacheth," he must not be surprised to hear the old answer, "Jesus I know, and Thomas Cook I know; but who are ye?"

No preacher will succeed by *merely* saying "Come;" and he who thinks that herein is the secret of Mr. Cook's success is greatly mistaken. Mr. Cook is in the habit of saying, that for an evangelist to succeed three things are required: Faith in God, faith in himself, and faith in his mission.

Even in the world much is accomplished by men who believe in themselves, and hence it is commonly said, "They *can*, who believe they can." A man knows, for example, whether or not he can drive four-in-hand, whether or not he can scale a high building, whether or not he can jump with safety off a running tram-car; and, as a rule, if he believes he can do these things, he is able to do them.

> "Our doubts are traitors,
> And make us lose the good we oft might win
> By fearing to attempt."

In the Christian Church the same remarks hold good. Given a man who firmly believes that for this purpose God has raised him up, that he may call sinners to repentance, and his ministry will be irresistible. Mr. Cook is as truly convinced that God has raised him up, and sent him to "do the work of an evangelist," as he is convinced that God raised up Moses and sent him to deliver the children of Israel from the hand of Pharaoh. And herein lies his great strength. Mr. Cook, accordingly, never preaches without expecting that God will work with him, and that signs will follow; and, as a matter of fact, it is so; and hence, whilst during the last ten years he has held, on an average, three hundred evangelistic services a year, he has not held more than a dozen out of the three thousand which have not borne visible fruit. The one idea of his life is to save men. He has no reputation to nurse, and, being a servant of Christ, he does not "please men." He has no pulpit dignity to maintain, but makes everything bend to the one purpose of leading sinners to Christ. A few years ago he was invited, during the sessions of the Irish Conference, to preach on the Sunday evening in the Conference chapel. The occasion was not wanting in importance, but the Evangelist selected one of his earliest sermons for the service, of which he afterwards told me he was ashamed, choosing it simply because it was one which God had much used for the conversion of sinners. The sermon did nothing to enhance his reputation, but it was the means of bringing fifty persons to decision, and thus it caused the "raptured songs above" to swell with increased joy over the new triumphs which the Saviour's Name wrought. Great sermons, it is to be feared, are often great sins; and if preachers would ask themselves before preaching them their reason for selecting them, such sermons would often be rejected instead of chosen.

Happily, Mr. Cook has no "great sermons." He has, however, some which have been owned of God more than others; and these he loves to preach, not because they increase his reputation every time they are repeated,—for this they do not do,—but because they are the means of "turning many to righteousness."

When Mr. Cook was a candidate for the ministry, his preaching was objected to on the ground that it was "too colloquial." But he has continued to adopt a colloquial style, and it should seem that the event has justified his decision. No doubt God can do as well without a slip-shod and slovenly style as He can do without the style of "Blair's Rhetoric." The evangelist should not offer to God that which costs him nothing. If a young mission-worker, with his eye on the ministry as his ultimate destination, thinks that because God cares nothing for human eloquence, he may justifiably be careless of his grammar and composition, and may so preach as to set all the School Board children in his congregation in a titter, he is seriously mistaken. The prophet Malachi says, "If ye offer the blind for sacrifice, is it not evil? And if ye offer the lame and the sick, is it not evil? Offer it now unto thy Governor; will He be pleased with thee, or accept thy person? saith the Lord of Hosts."

The editors of magazines and of newspapers would not be "pleased" with us if we were to offer them some of the compositions which we offer to God. "Scamped" work ill becomes the pulpit. John Bright was not born a ready-made orator, but took infinite pains to acquire his matchless style, which enabled him to be understood by the Birmingham artisans, and at the same time charmed the ear of the fastidious. Would to God that more preachers had a style calculated to compel the indolent to listen, and to prevent the critic from scoffing! Gold and frankincense and myrrh are fitting gifts for the Son of God.

All this it seemed necessary to say lest we should encourage mental indolence; and, having found courage to write it, we may now add without fear of being misunderstood, that Thomas Cook has always endeavoured to use great plainness of speech, and to avoid what the *Spectator* has called "pulpit English." At the same time, like "such an one as Paul," he has never been guilty of buffoonery and vulgarity, but has spoken the mystery of Christ as he ought to speak it, and, consequently, with much acceptance to many of the most intelligent congregations in Methodism.

An evangelist can be plain without being coarse, simple without being foolish.

Mr. Cook endeavours to be as personal in his preaching as it is possible for him to be, seeing that usually he preaches to strangers with whose sins and habits he has no special acquaintance. To what purpose is it that we "smite the Agnostics hip and thigh, and pour lava upon the Mormons who are thousands of miles away," and have nothing to say to the man in the nearest pew? Preaching to absentees will be bootless. "Thou art the man" is the style of the successful preacher, who causes his hearer to be, not pleased with the preacher, but displeased with himself. On one occasion when our Evangelist was preaching at Croydon, a seat-holder abruptly left during the service, remarking at the door to some onlooker, "That man ought to be imprisoned for preaching like that." But, as Mr. Moody was wont to say when in this country, there is hope of a man who is made angry by the Word.

Like Finney, Mr. Cook believes in repeating his main points until he has got them imbedded in the minds of his hearers. It may be remembered that Finney quotes a judge, who remarked to him that preachers make a mistake in not doing as advocates do, whose habit it is to repeat over their main positions about as many times as there are men in the jury-box. Lawyers would ruin their cause if they were afraid of repetition; Thomas Cook gains his cause by not being afraid of the same thing. "One tenpenny nail," says Mr. Spurgeon, "driven home, and clinched, will be more useful than a score of tin-tacks loosely fixed, to be pulled up again in an hour."

He also seeks to persuade men, and "beseeches" them to be reconciled to God. Dr. Dale has truly said, that "to leave the truth to do its own work, and to trust to the hearts and consciences of our hearers to apply it, is a great and fatal mistake." That mistake our Evangelist strenuously avoids. Nor is his ministry without the element of fear. The temper of the times is opposed to the sterner aspects of the gospel, and people generally are intolerant of all teaching that insists upon the future punishment of sin. Present-day preachers, especially Methodist preachers, may well ask themselves whether or not they are as much in earnest in warning sinners to flee from the wrath to come, as were their fathers, particularly the early Methodist preachers.

Dr. Dale, who, it has been well said, is the preacher's preacher, as Shelley was the poet's poet, in his *Old Evangelicalism and New*, asks this pertinent question: "Are we as *anxious*, ministers and people, about men as our fathers were? On any theory of eschatology there is a dark and menacing future for those who have been brought face to face with Christ in this life, and have refused to receive His salvation, and to submit to His authority. I do not ask whether the element of fear has a great place in our *preaching*, but whether it has a great place in our *hearts*—whether we ourselves are afraid—whether the Christian people who have been trained by us are afraid—of what will come to men who do not believe in Christ; whether we, whether our people, are filled with an agonising earnestness for their salvation." To use the language of a deeply-thoughtful Christian writer, "The thin and washy versions of Christianity current in our day" have no room for the element of fear, and have no severe condemnation for the sins of poor men. And yet it is written, "The Lord Jesus shall be revealed from heaven with His mighty angels, in flaming fire taking vengeance on them that know not God, and that obey not the gospel of our Lord Jesus Christ; who shall be punished with everlasting destruction from the presence of the Lord, and from the glory of His power." Men will not, in numberless cases, go to Christ, "our Deliverer from the wrath to come," unless they realise that out of Christ the wrath of God abideth on them; and therefore, while it is perfectly true, as Mr. Moody once said, that "a preacher ought to have a very tender heart to speak with good effect about the condition of the lost," it is equally true that every preacher should "put on a heart of compassion" (R.V.); and the love of Christ should constrain him,—

> "With cries, entreaties, *tears*, to save,
> To snatch them from the gaping grave."

Some of Mr. Cook's success is due to this element having a considerable place in his ministry.

The expectation of immediate results is another principle of Mr. Cook's ministry. Some preachers fail to secure their object because they do not expect to succeed, and would really be as much astonished if they did, as Peter was astonished when his "nets enclosed a great multitude of fishes."

Mr. Cook fully expects that the Divine blessing will accompany the Word; but his faith is not always shared by his fellow-labourers, and therefore it often happens that one of his first duties in beginning a mission is to awaken faith in God's people. On one occasion, when the Evangelist met the workers on the Saturday evening previous to the first Sunday, he gave thanks, as he often does, for the victories about to be achieved. At the close of the service an unbelieving brother remarked, "But how will it be, Mr. Cook, if no good is done?" "I am not going to suppose any such thing," was the Evangelist's reply; "good is sure to be done."

Often when he has gone to a church for a single Sunday, he has found the people quite destitute of all expectation of visible fruit, especially if the occasion has been a Sunday-school anniversary. In such cases he will excite a spirit of hopefulness by asking the stewards to prepare sheets of paper on which the names of the inquirers may be written, and to prepare vestries for their accommodation in the after-meeting. Then he will boldly make the collection before the sermon, in order that nothing may frustrate his purpose at the close of the service; and never does he leave the chapel without drawing the net to the shore. Sometimes he has had to contend with organists and choirs who have been bent on musical performances, and whose sympathy with his object has been but slight. A while ago, for instance, he went to a watering-place to preach on the Sunday, and found on arriving at the chapel that a distinguished musician was expecting to give an organ recital at the close of the evening service. Such an arrangement would have been fatal to the Evangelist's one great design, and he felt bound to forbid it being carried out. The stewards pleaded for the programme to be followed, but the Evangelist was inexorable, and the result was that while the eminent player was displeased, "the Lord added to the Church" that evening twenty souls who were "being saved." Mr. Cook has often found that some of the best converts of a mission have been the hardest to win, and it is therefore a principle with him not to lose heart, but by the use of all means to seek to save some, as was the custom of that great soul-winner St. Paul. Not seldom our Evangelist's faith has been sorely tried. Upon one occasion he told the congregation before the sermon was finished that God had given him the assurance that souls would be saved at that service, and he was therefore confident of victory. When he had concluded his sermon, he appealed to his hearers to come out and avow themselves on the Lord's side. But there was no response. He renewed his appeal, being persuaded that God would not fail him. Five, ten, twenty minutes passed, and still there was no answer made to his entreaty; and it was suggested to the Evangelist that God was going to fail him, and put him to shame before the congregation. For a moment the perspiration stood on his brow, but faith soon conquered, and he was convinced that heaven and earth might pass away, but God's word must be fulfilled. He therefore said to the people, "If you do not come, God has not sent me; but if God has sent me, come you will." He then waited to see what God would do. For some moments perfect stillness prevailed, and a sacred awe seemed to rest upon the congregation. Then the power of God was felt. Many bowed their heads and wept, while numbers of persons rose in all parts of the chapel and wended their way to the inquiry-rooms, and all present said,

"We have seen strange things to-day." It need scarcely be said that no prudent man of God will adopt such a course as this except under special circumstances. No such man will resolve beforehand to proceed in this way, nor will any wise evangelist ever dare to imitate this procedure, unless he also, like Mr. Cook, is convinced that he is being led by the Spirit of God. "And the Lord said, Shall I hide from *Abraham* that thing which I do?" "The secret of the Lord is with them that fear Him." "If thine eye be single, thy whole body shall be full of light."

In almost every mission there are hearers present who apparently will never be won by public preaching, but who will yield to personal entreaty. On the other hand, there are others who would resent any personal attempt that was made to bring them to decision, and who, therefore, must be approached only from the pulpit. He that winneth souls is wise enough to discriminate between these classes, and to vary his methods according to the peculiarities of his hearers, and not commit himself to any stereotyped form of procedure. Every evangelist should combine the fullest common sense with the deepest fervour. He who was ready to "die at Jerusalem for the name of the Lord Jesus," was content to become "all things to all men."

After pleading for an hour one evening with a young fellow who seemed utterly indifferent, the Evangelist, as he was leaving him, asked God to enable him to speak one final word that might bring the man to decision. Then turning to him Mr. Cook said, "Do not think you will be doing God a favour by yielding to His offers; He can do very well without you." The rebuke was effectual. The next night that young man was a humble penitent.

> "Words which Thou Thyself shalt give me,
> Must prevail."

On another occasion, a gentleman of much refinement attended every service during a mission, but would not surrender to God. The last evening came, and still he held out. Some of the workers would fain have spoken to him in his pew, but the Evangelist prohibited them from doing so, having a premonition that for them to do so would be for them to defeat their purpose. But as the final service was just about to be closed, Mr. Cook walked down the aisle to the gentleman in question, and, asking God to give him the right word, touched him on the shoulder and quietly said, "If you are not in the kingdom, but desire to be, follow me," and then walked away. The gentleman instantly rose and followed the Evangelist to the inquiry room, and that night he began a new life.

Tactics such as these must be used by evangelists who would succeed, but they cannot be learned as military science may be. The art of winning souls is acquired on the knees. He who would do much *for* God must needs be much *with* God.

In some places it is found that singing-bands are useful in arresting public attention and increasing the congregations; in other places they are a waste of time and strength. The great point which the evangelist has to consider is, how he can best adapt his methods to the particular church which he is endeavouring to revive and increase. Mr. Cook has published some "Hints on Preparation" which he usually sends in advance to the places he is about to visit, and which prove very serviceable. A large choir always proves a source of great attraction. At some of Mr. Cook's missions the choir has been two hundred and fifty strong, and then it has rendered most efficient service. It is also found highly advantageous to precede the mission by a week of prayer. Indirectly this does immense good. It excites expectation; it tends to fasten attention upon individuals; and it quickens effort, for most people feel, when they have prayed, that it behoves them to second their prayers with their endeavours. The direct consequences of a week of prayer are incalculable. Mr. Cook encourages the Lord's people to make out a prayer-list, on which they write the names of a dozen persons in whose conversion they are particularly interested, and for whom they pledge themselves to pray. Thus they concentrate thought and prayer upon individuals, instead of merely taking a sort of general interest in the work. This tends to secure definiteness in prayer. Instead of only praying in private for the conversion of sinners in general, the workers who comply with this rule intercede for particular persons, and then seek to promote their object by inviting the persons to the mission and speaking directly to them when a suitable opportunity occurs. There must be much latent praying power in the Churches, and this the successful evangelist will always endeavour to develope. We solicit subscriptions on behalf of others; we ask for self-sacrificing efforts on behalf of others; why not ask for prayers for others? It will often be seen that some who, on account of age, or sickness, or extreme poverty, can do nothing else for a mission, can render the best possible help by pleading alone with God for its success. "The poor of this world" can indeed render invaluable service when they are "rich in faith."

One of the less important means which, if judiciously used, contributes a good deal to promote the success of a mission, is the local newspaper press. Handbills may or may not be read, but everybody reads the newspaper, and hence a paragraph inserted in the local paper is of great service. Sometimes, if the representatives of the press are courteously approached, they will write "leaders" on the mission, or cause them to be written, or if written by one of the friends of the mission they will insert them, and thereby greatly help to make the mission known, and to bring it into favour.

The wisdom of the serpent is as necessary as the harmlessness of the dove. The evangelist must always remember Wesley's words, and have all his wits about him.

The holiness meetings, held in the afternoons, are always of great value in furthering the success of the mission. This will appear later on, and need not now be referred to at length.

At the evening services "repentance toward God" is insisted upon, and hearers are urged to leave their sins as well as their pews in order that they may find God. The Evangelist discourages the workers from speaking to people in their pews, and relies on the penitents coming out voluntarily as inquirers. Indeed, nothing in Mr. Cook's missions is so remarkable as the spontaneous way in which the converts, as a rule, stand up to be prayed for by the preacher, and then come out of their pews and enter the rooms prepared for their reception. It is no uncommon thing for all the workers to be directed by the Evangelist to proceed to the inquiry-rooms, and to do this before any converts have discovered their intention to do the same. But in these instances the workers have been quickly followed by the penitents, and the circumstance is only stated here in order to show that it is not a principle with him to put undue pressure upon his hearers, and to force them into the inquiry-rooms *nolens volens*.

It is generally known that Mr. Cook conducts his after-meetings in a manner quite contrary to the traditions of the elders, sometimes taking all the burden upon himself, and perhaps even closing a service without prayer having been publicly offered excepting by himself. He believes, however, that by arranging continually during the services for silent prayer to be offered, as a matter of fact more prayer ascends to heaven during his missions than there would if he followed the ordinary method; and as he usually does not know many of the men who might be likely to lead the prayers of the congregations if the meetings were thrown open, he is of opinion that his plan safeguards his services from the interposition of unsuitable persons, and is the best possible method for *him*, whether or not it may be so for others.

It must not be supposed, however, that our Evangelist undervalues the prayers of God's people. On the contrary, he esteems them very highly, and encourages the praying people to "continue steadfastly in prayer" at all times, and especially during the mission. The congregations are invited to send requests for prayer, and these are read by the Evangelist and remembered by him publicly and audibly when he leads the devotions of the people, and by the congregation during the intervals allowed for private prayer.

As we have seen, workers are directed to draw up lists of names of persons for whom they promise to offer special private prayer; and it is no uncommon thing for friends to send requests for praise to be offered before the mission closes, because all the persons whose names were on their lists have been brought to God.

Whilst holding a mission in South Wales, Mr. Cook was asked to plead with God especially for a young fellow who had been trained in a godly home, but had become utterly careless and prayerless. This young man treated the mission as a huge joke, and defied his friends to influence him by their prayers. The Evangelist and his co-workers prayed that the man might be led to come to the men's meetings. He positively refused to come, and made up his mind to have a quiet Sunday afternoon at home with his books and his pipe. As he lived near the chapel he was able to watch the men go in, and as the time for beginning the service drew near, it struck him that he would go to his window and see who was going. This he did, and he was surprised to observe many unlikely men entering the chapel—prominent tradesmen, professional men, and others. His curiosity was excited. "I wonder what sort of a meeting it will be! I've a good mind to creep in at the back and see." So he said to himself, and he acted accordingly. When he entered the chapel he found the back seats occupied, and he was obliged to walk higher up than he intended to do. As he bowed his head for private prayer, a strange feeling came over him; and when he raised his head, instead of rising on his feet and joining in singing, he made his way direct to the inquiry-room, crying for mercy. Before the Evangelist began his address that afternoon the young man was rejoicing in God's forgiving love.

Let the reader add to this incident from Wales another from Lincolnshire. A lady came to the Evangelist at the seven o'clock Sunday morning prayer-meeting, and said, "Oh, Mr. Cook, I have had a great disappointment. I have been praying for years for the conversion of my husband; especially have I done this of late since I heard you were coming here to hold a mission. I thought it very likely that during these services he would be saved; and now, two days ago, he was called away to Cambridge, where he will remain all the time you are here."

"But," said the Evangelist, "God can reach him at Cambridge. Let us ask Him to do so." Thereupon a few persons joined in prayer for the husband. That very day, as it afterwards transpired, the prayer was answered. The man being away from home felt lonely that Sunday, and did not know what to do with himself. In the morning he turned in at the Wesleyan Chapel, but he was not as much helped by the service as he expected. In the evening, as he chanced to pass the Baptist Chapel, something said to him, "Go in there," and accordingly in he went. It proved to be an evangelistic service; the preacher had just the message for him, and there and then the man believed and was saved. Another case may be mentioned of a like kind. This happened in our greatest seat of learning, Oxford, and it was on this wise. An elderly widow woman sought and found the Lord at the mission, and then, as was most natural, she instantly became concerned for her son, who was a soldier, and who, having been ordered abroad, was to sail the following week. "If only he was saved," said the good mother, "I should be willing to let him go. Do pray for him." The request was, of course, granted, and the answer came in the following way. Greatly to the mother's surprise, the son, who was the servant of an officer, came home on the following Saturday, leave having been given him to spend a few days with his mother before he went abroad. The mother brought her lad with her to the service on the Sunday evening, and amongst the first to respond to the preacher's appeal was the soldier boy, who came forward and soon found the blessing which he sought. "He can go abroad now," said the widowed mother; "if we don't meet again on earth, we shall meet in heaven."

"Coincidences" these circumstances will be called by persons who know nothing of the possibilities of prayer; "direct answers to prayer" they will be called by those who know "the secret of the Lord."

Much has already been said about the inquiry-room, and as the use of the inquiry-room forms one of Mr. Cook's chief methods, some remarks thereon may be useful.

In early Methodism the Sunday evening prayer-meeting was unknown. Probably John Smith, whom I once heard Dr. Osborn describe as the most successful of all Methodist evangelists, and John Rattenbury, must be held responsible for the introduction of this comparatively modern arrangement; certainly before their day it was unknown. Thus, by way of example, it may be said that when Dr. Bunting travelled in the Grosvenor Street Circuit, Manchester, he had the great happiness to see the membership of the Circuit doubled in three years. And yet he never held a Sunday night prayer-meeting, nor did he ever have "a mission." The result was effected in this way. The Word of God was powerfully preached, and the Holy Ghost bore testimony to the Word of His grace. Large sacramental services and Society meetings were held. The week-evening services were well attended. And the Lord's people were always on the alert for hearers convinced of sin, whom they took by the hand and led to the class-meeting, the leader taking care that such persons should not remain in bondage, but should be helped to obtain the blessing of justification. The class-meetings were therefore originally used very largely for distinctively evangelistic purposes, and this explains why it is that in the "Directions" addressed to leaders and printed in the class-books, and—shall we say?—read by every class-leader, care is taken to instruct the leader to mark every name on his book in the proper column, so as to indicate to the pastor when he examines the class-book the spiritual *state* of the members. If the member is living in the enjoyment of justification, his name should be marked thus, "o." If he is a penitent who is seeking for salvation, but does not enjoy living faith in Christ, his name should be marked thus, "a."

A revival of this custom has long seemed to us to

be desirable, and it is recommended in the prize essay on the class-meeting by the Rev. Simpson Johnson, in a suggestive paragraph, marked "Make the class-meeting an aggressive agency." In modern Methodism the custom is to invite persons convinced of sin to stand up publicly, or to go forward to the penitent form, or to retire to the inquiry-room. Much may be said for and against these methods; but from the day of Pentecost to the present day evangelists have deemed it necessary to insist upon some test whereby persons who are convinced of sin may prove to themselves and to others that such is the case. In the days of the apostles baptism served this purpose. "They that gladly received [Peter's] word were baptized," and they that were not baptized did not receive his word. Thus the distinction was broad and clear, and the converts avowed their "new creation" in the most marked manner. Seeing, however, that evangelists now usually preach to baptized persons, it is not open to them to use that method, and they are obliged to have recourse to another.

As a matter of fact our hearers are "being saved" (Acts ii. 47, R.V) or they "are perishing" (2 Cor. iv. 3, R.V.), and what is wanted is to ascertain their exact condition. Furthermore, it is not possible to pray definitely for anxious souls, and to give them suitable counsel, unless they disclose their anxiety in some way, and give the workers the means of advising them. The inquiry-room method promotes these ends, and it also enables the penitent to cross the rubicon, and to put his hand deliberately to the plough. It is a public intimation to his friends, and often to boon companions, who must needs be shaken off, that the penitent has "cast off the works of darkness and put on the armour of light." And this method brings the inquirer and the well-instructed and sympathetic Christian worker face to face, and thus facilitates the actual conversion of many whose knowledge of "the way of God" is most imperfect.

Whatever the reader may think of this method of evangelism, it will remain true that God has sanctioned it most markedly by His blessing, and that it has promoted the conversion of thousands of persons who had remained in their pews for years without experiencing any saving change of heart.

The inquiry-room has some advantages over the penitent form, and, indeed, in large crowded missions the latter is an impossible method. Needful quiet is obtained in the inquiry-room; intelligent instruction can then be given to individuals, who may answer as well as ask questions; and suitable workers can be selected for particular persons. As a rule, the two sexes are directed to go to separate rooms, and Christian men are sent to the men's room and Christian women to the other room. Mr. Cook's plan is to invite workers and penitents to come out together, and by so doing the cross is made a little lighter for the more timid ones. And while he earnestly bids his unsaved hearers to adopt this course, he is careful to make it appear that a refusal to do so is not tantamount to the rejection of Christ.

When the converts have entered the inquiry-room, they all kneel down, and the workers also, for prayer. The room is usually in charge of a minister, and he will generally offer a short prayer, and then give out a verse for all to sing. The converts are requested to kneel and the workers to stand, and then the minister, who is supposed to know every one, and, as the pastor, is most competent for the office, assigns to each penitent a suitable "worker." If there are more "workers" than are needed, the unemployed ones either return to the chapel or quietly wait to see if more penitents will come, spending the time in private prayer. The "workers" are instructed pretty much to the following effect:—Find out where the inquirer is. Diagnose the case. Do not pry into details, but ascertain the present condition of the person committed to your charge. Get the convert to talk to you before you speak much to him. Do not assume that every "inquirer" is an awakened sinner. Do not attach too much importance to weeping. Some weep the most whose convictions are the weakest, and some do not weep at all, who nevertheless have set their face like a flint against sin. Willingness to forsake sin and to accept the will of God is the proper test of repentance. Do not speak of faith until you have good reason to believe that the inquirer has repented of his sins. Use the Word of God. Direct the inquirers to the finished work of Christ. Do not say, "Only believe!" but tell them clearly *what* to believe. Do not occupy their attention with the thought of believing. It is not faith, but Christ that saves. Give them to see their personal interest in the atonement of the Lord Jesus Christ. Take them where St. Paul was when he said, "The Son of God loved *me*, and gave Himself for *me*." In this way you will find some commit themselves to faith not knowing that they are doing so, and they will be astonished to find that they *are* saved, because they have accepted the work of Christ, and God has accepted them for Christ's sake. Never ask inquirers how they *feel*. To do that is to direct attention *within*, whereas they must look *without* if they are to obtain comfort and salvation. In using your own experience, be careful to avoid laying it down as a rule which must be followed in other cases. Give the Spirit of God play for variety. Never pronounce judgment upon an individual. Leave the Holy Spirit to assure of pardon as He has convinced of sin. Do not talk too much. Fussy "workers" weaken good impressions. Do not move about from one inquirer to another, but remain with the one first committed to you. For several persons to speak to one inquirer, and especially for more than one to speak at the same time, is most confusing. After you have made the way of salvation as plain as you can, leave the penitent to transact his own business with God, kneeling quietly by his side, and warding away other workers who may be disposed to speak to him, but whose words at the present moment would darken counsel. Do not talk loudly so as to disturb others, and do not pray audibly nor sing. When singing is desirable, or audible prayer, the minister in charge will give directions to that effect, and, as much depends upon order and quiet, his wishes must be carried out. Persevere with your case, and do not heal the wound slightly. Far better it will be to let the penitent go away uncomforted than to send him away resting on a false foundation. Some of the most difficult cases will prove to be the best. Do not merely tell your inquirers of the comforts of religion, but prepare them for its trials, that they may have "root in themselves," to use our Lord's fine figure, and not fall away when persecution or affliction arises because of the Word.

After the workers have done their part in the inquiry-room, the Evangelist usually sums up, taking typical cases and dealing with them, answering objections, correcting errors, and leading the inquirers as a body into the way of peace. No work is more important than that of instructing inquirers, and "workers" should prepare themselves for this solemn duty by studying the Word of God, and especially those parts which refer to this subject, and also by reading such booklets as the Rev. J. G. Stuart's *Dealing with Anxious Persons*, and Mr. Aitken's *Difficulties with the Soul*.

Members of County Councils and of School Boards read much literature in order to qualify themselves for the duties of their offices. Members of Christian Churches should also *take pains* to qualify themselves for the discharge of their more important duties, that "the King should have no damage."

The reader may be interested in a letter addressed to the present writer by the Rev. W Allen (C.), who writes thus: "I took Mr. Cook on the Saturday evening to see the chapel in which he was to hold the mission. He asked at once, 'Where is the inquiry-room?' adding, 'when I ask the anxious ones to-morrow night to stand up, I must know where to direct them to go.' 'Oh,' I said, 'but you will not ask any one to stand up until the after-meeting, shall you?' 'Yes,' was his reply; 'I hope to see several persons rise in different parts of the chapel at the close of my sermon.' This appeared to me so unusual for Yarmouth, that a hundred fears rushed into my mind at once; for I thought it would prejudice the mission, especially in the minds of members of other Churches. I moved my hand towards his arm, intending to expostulate with him, when it was suggested to me that I ought not to interfere with one who was being led by the Spirit of God.

"How thankful I felt on the following evening that I did not interfere! When the chapel was crowded, he proceeded to 'draw in the net;' and about forty persons rose in proof that they had decided to serve God, and these, with others, afterwards entered the inquiry-rooms. The total number of inquirers at Yarmouth in that mission was three hundred and sixty, a very large proportion of which number belonged to other Churches.

"Mr. Cook was then nine years younger than he is now, and very youthful in appearance. I had prepared the people in some measure for a young mission preacher; but when some of them saw the Evangelist for the first time, they were not a little surprised. He was not, however, immature, not devoid of power, but a master of assemblies. I never witnessed greater control exercised over meetings, or a wiser management of crowded congregations, than during that mission."

The late Rev. Alexander M'Aulay writes, under date February 17th, 1885: "Your account of the Walsall mission exalts one's hope of more abundant manifestations of the Holy Spirit everywhere. It confirms my strongly-expressed conviction that Methodism is paralysed by substituting many means and agencies for simple faith in the power of the Holy Spirit, and the foolishness of preaching. God will work only in His own way, and slay with His own weapons. The heavenly power that saves a collier in the Black Country will save a student in Oxford. May this saving power not be hindered by unbelief! Self and sect are twin nurses of unbelief."

Methods are, however, of secondary importance. The great matter is to obtain that enduement of power without which evangelists and "workers" are criminally weak. The reconversion of the Church must precede the conversion of the masses of the people; and perhaps it would be well for the Church to cease to make weak efforts to reach "them that are without" until the Church has received that blessing to which our Lord referred when He said, "Ye shall receive power, after that the Holy Ghost is come upon you; and ye shall be witnesses unto Me both in Jerusalem, and in Judea, and in Samaria, and unto the uttermost part of the earth." [1]

[1] Whilst these pages are passing through the press, the Methodist Churches throughout the world are giving themselves to prayer in a remarkable manner, and there are indications of a coming revival. May God rend the heavens and come down, that the mountains may flow down at His presence!

CHAPTER VII.

HOLINESS-MEETINGS.

FROM the first, Mr. Cook has been led to give great prominence to the doctrine of scriptural holiness. Always have holiness-meetings been a prominent feature of his missions, and very richly have these services been blessed to the people of God. Hence this aspect of his early ministry deserves close attention.

As we have seen, Mr. Cook became impressed with the importance of this great truth shortly after his conversion, and he was soon made a conscious partaker of "the fulness of God." His own experience has confirmed the theory which he adopted in the beginning of his Christian career, which was to the effect that, to be specially useful in the work of God, it is needful to be fully cleansed from "sin's offensive stain," and to be endued with power from on high.

There is reason to believe that the Methodist doctrine of entire sanctification is not well understood by the members of other Churches, many of whom are like a working-man to whom I once gave a Society-class ticket, and who said, in his own vernacular, that he heard his mates talk about the second blessing—he didn't understand it, but if it "licked the first, it would be a grand 'un."

Dr. Dale understands the doctrine, and consequently accepts it, and sees in it the possibility of an ethical reformation of greater importance than the doctrinal reformation of the sixteenth century. Mr. Spurgeon does not fully understand it, and hence sometimes feels it right to dispute about it,—as, for example, he once did in my hearing, when he remarked that "some people say that in them sin is dead; but if that be so, I am sure that sin is not buried in them; and," he added, with characteristic delight over a smart saying, "I warrant that, if you were to live with these people, you would find that it has a remarkable smell in many of these individuals." We cherish no feeling of resentment towards Mr. Spurgeon for this somewhat vulgar observation; for we are sure that when he made it, although he possibly was enjoying the blessing, he certainly did not understand it. The Rev. Dr. Mackennal, however, appears to comprehend it; for in addressing the Wesleyan-Methodist Conference in Manchester in the year 1887, he declared that for nothing would the Churches of this country thank the Wesleyan-Methodist Church more than for bearing constant testimony to this truth, that holiness is imparted to the soul of the believer by the direct gift of God.

To this momentous doctrine Mr. Cook has continued to bear faithful witness from the first; and the result is, that thousands of believers have been raised up who witness that the blood of Jesus Christ, God's Son, cleanses them from all sin.

To object to Mr. Cook's holiness-meetings on the ground that all our services are intended to spread holiness, is a mere quibble. The class-meeting was always intended to be a fellowship-meeting; and yet the early Methodists deemed it proper to have their band-meetings in addition,—a custom which was so good, that we much regret the discontinuance of it.

As the subject is of the greatest interest, I will subjoin an address which I heard Mr. Cook deliver not many months ago, and which he has since published in a small booklet, entitled *Entire Cleansing*, only adding, that it may be accepted as an embodiment of the Evangelist's views, and of the teaching which he has given during the last ten years in all parts of the country :—

"*The blood of Jesus Christ, His Son, cleanseth us from all sin.*"—1 John i. 7

"The reason why many do not apprehend the true nature of the salvation of Jesus Christ, is because they do not understand the true nature of sin. Defective views of sin lead to incorrect views of privilege. Only when our views are cleared as to sin do we rise to a full appreciation of the salvation Christ has purchased for us.

"There are two primary aspects under which it may be viewed. Sin is wrong-doing; but a state of sinfulness existed before we began to do. Wrong-doing involves guilt, and needs forgiveness; but a state of sinfulness cannot be forgiven; this is removed by cleansing.

"We shall not understand this subject unless we keep in mind this twofold character of sin. We must discriminate between guilt and depravity. Depravity is not actual sin; it is the inward fountain from which actual sins originate. Sin committed is the transgression of the law, but depravity is in-born, inherited. It lies deeper down and farther back than wrong-doing. It is sin in embryo—that state of the heart out of which acts of sin are born. It manifests itself in a bias towards evil, 'a bent to sinning' in a proneness to depart from God. Forgiveness refers to actions, but depravity is not action: it is a state. God's plan is to cleanse it away.

"Let me illustrate what I mean: A mother puts upon her child a clean pinafore, and says, 'Now this is not to be soiled.' But the child disobeys. She may forgive the child for her disobedience, but she cannot forgive the pinafore clean; she must wash it. So God may forgive the wrong that we do, but He cannot forgive a depraved heart. Heart-sin must be cleansed away, and it is to this cleansing the text refers—'The blood of Jesus Christ, His Son, cleanseth us from all sin.'

"There are many scriptures which teach this twofold aspect of salvation. Zechariah represents the fountain of atonement as furnishing pardon for sin (guilt), and purity for uncleanness (depravity). St. John's teaching is just the same: 'God is faithful and just to forgive us our sins (guilt), and to cleanse us from all unrighteousness' (depravity). And with this view our hymn is in perfect accord: 'the water and the blood' symbolise this 'double cure,' 'save from wrath, and make me pure.'

"The whole tenor of Scripture teaches that the purpose of the death of Christ was not to save us from the consequences of sin merely, but to save us from sin itself—the sin which causes the sins. It is this being, or 'body of sin,' as St. Paul terms it, that is to be 'crucified' and 'destroyed,' in order that 'henceforth we may not serve sin' (Rom. vi. 6).

"The divine method is not to lop off a branch here and cut away an excrescence there, but to strike at the root.

"We read recently of a man who said he had cured his boy of pilfering, and on being asked how he had done it, he said he had tied his hands behind his back! It need scarcely be said that this is not the way in which God works. He does more than make men moral. Morality is doing right in spite of strong inclinations towards wrong, but holiness takes away every 'want to' that inclines towards the wrong, and turns all our desires towards that which is good. Hands do not steal; there is something behind the hands. Some will say there is the will; but our nature is behind our will, and it is there where God would put us right. Better than his creed he may be, but no man is better than his heart. If sin be in us in some form or another, it will come out. It is only by removing the cause that the effect will cease.

"Does not the high import of the Sermon on the Mount consist in the fact, that a moral condition is demanded antecedent to the act? Not only is the external observance of the ten commandments required, but the secret desires of the heart must also be pure. Most persons are dead to the sin of murder as an act, *i.e.* they have never lifted their hand to strike the fatal blow; but St. John teaches: 'He that hateth his brother is a murderer,'—that those who cherish feelings of malice or desires for revenge are as certainly guilty as those who have committed the deed. The law is as surely broken by the man who would sin if he dared, as in the case of him whose state of heart finds expression in outward acts. The 'want to' sin is sin. There is a point between the earth and the moon where the direction of the action of gravitation changes. If we could hurl a missile with sufficient force that it would reach that point, instead of coming back to earth, in the superior attraction of the moon, it would rush with increasing velocity to meet it. This illustrates human experience when the law of the 'spirit of life in Christ Jesus' makes us free from the 'law of sin and death.' The natural tendency in us towards sin (the law of sin and death) is not only neutralised and counteracted when the Holy Spirit comes to the heart in sanctifying power (the law of the spirit of life), but under the more powerful operation of this latter law the soul now gravitates upwards. Every aspiration is now Godward, and His service a luxury and a delight. The 'want to' that inclined us towards evil is now taken away, and every desire is towards that which is good. That this is not the experience of all Christians I need hardly say. Conversion and full cleansing of the heart from sin scarcely ever take place at the same time. It is by no means uncommon for persons to imagine at the time of forgiveness that sin is not only pardoned but destroyed. The change is so great, even as 'from death unto life,' that the work of moral renovation seems perfect. But soon high-wrought emotions subside; the petty annoyances of life begin to chafe; temptations from the devil assail; and then their mistake is discovered. They find that the old man is bound only, not cast out. They have dominion over sin, but they are not dead to it. It is suspended, held in check, repressed, but it is not fully cleansed from the soul. It does not reign, but it exists. It was this consciousness of the presence of sin in his heart that led the Indian to say to the missionary a short time after his conversion—'I feel as if there were two Indians in me, a good Indian and a bad Indian.' We would not for a moment minify the great work of conversion; but all experience testifies that an 'infection of nature' does remain warring against the spirit, even in those who are regenerate. It is a state of mixedness: a sort of duality exists within, in which the flesh and the spirit antagonise each other; and this is manifestly only a temporary condition; because sooner or later one or the other of these opposing principles must be expelled. In cleansing the heart from all sin, God eliminates from the mixture all the elements which antagonise the elements of holiness planted in regeneration. He casts out all the buyers and sellers from the temple. He excludes all the Canaanites from the land. He delivers us 'from all our enemies, that we may serve Him without fear, in holiness and righteousness before Him all the days of our life.' When this is done the conflict within ceases. The soul enters upon the Sabbath rest of the love of God, and is filled with 'perfect peace.'

"The difference between conversion and purity of heart has been well illustrated as follows: In the coal regions of Wyoming Valley, in America, there are two principal seams of coal, which lie one above the other. In the first and upper seam, while there is a great preponderance of coal, there are little seams of slate running all through the coal. The lower seam, however, is much thicker, and is all pure solid coal, without a single seam of slate. The upper seam resembles the regenerate heart, in which there is a preponderance of grace; but the rudiments of sin, antagonising grace, are also there. The lower seam resembles Christian experience under the cleansing power of the blood of Christ, when the pure love of God fills the heart, excluding all its opposites. Then the graces of the Spirit exist in the soul without alloy, without mixture, in simplicity.

"This entire cleansing of the soul from sin may also be described as purity of heart. There are various degrees of impurity, but, strictly speaking, there are no degrees of purity. According to Webster, the word 'pure' means 'entire separation from all heterogeneous and extraneous matter, clear, free from mixture, as pure water, pure air, pure silver, or gold.' The word translated 'pure' occurs about seventy times in the New Testament in some of its forms. We may get at the idea the word was meant to convey by noting how the original word has been used. It is used of a body not smeared with paint or ointment, of vines without excrescences, of wheat when all the chaff has been winnowed away, of gold in which there is no alloy. The idea is, that that which is pure consists of one thing: it is without mixture or adulteration. Where there is mixture there cannot be purity. A pure heart contains nothing adverse to God. The Psalmist prayed: 'Wash me, and I shall be whiter than snow.' This is no highly-wrought figure of speech. Scientific research has shown that snow is not absolutely pure. But when the blood of Jesus Christ cleanses us from all sin, our souls shall be 'whiter than snow.' Miss Havergal might well ask,

'If *all* does not mean *all*, pray what does it mean?' The expression '*all sin*' covers the whole ground, embracing the aggregate of the evil propensities, dispositions, and tendencies of the carnal nature; the whole of sin in man. Had the word '*all*' been omitted, we should have been puzzled to know from how much sin we could be saved, and from how much we could not. But this word settles the question, and leaves no doubt as to our privilege. 'The *blood of Jesus* cleanseth.' Alas, how many Christians limit the Holy One of Israel! Not a few have discrowned Christ as the Saviour, and are waiting for death to do what He cannot do. Our Bibles teach us of the time, the means, and the agent of sanctification; but nowhere is it taught that death is any of these. We do read that 'the last enemy to be destroyed is death;' but if death brings the destruction of sin, he can hardly be described as an 'enemy.' If this were true, instead of being the 'last enemy' he would be the last friend, and the best friend too. What is death? It is the separation of the soul from the body. But the mere separation of the soul from the body will not destroy sin in the soul; and only the soul can be the seat of sin.

"It is to be feared that those who have no expectation of full deliverance from sin until death comes to the help of Jesus, have got hold of a relic of Gnosticism,—a heresy which was early introduced into Christianity as a corrupting element. The Gnostics taught that in all matter was evil, ineradicable evil. Because our bodies are material matter, they believed there was therefore evil in our bodies; and because the spirit dwells in such a body, it is tainted, and must be, till this 'mortal puts on immortality.' But the idea of sin in the body is totally unscriptural, as it is palpably absurd. No body, or matter of any kind, can be sinful; spirits alone are capable of sin. To teach that our spirits will be cleansed from sin after death would involve the Papal error of purgatory

"The heart must be purified, therefore, in the moment of death, or before; and we have already shown the mere separation of the soul from the body will not effect this change. When, then, will this cleansing take place? Before death necessarily. And if it is the blood of Christ that cleanses from sin, why not now? God is as able and as willing to save from all sin now as He will be a moment before death. All Christians believe that the command, 'Thou shalt love the Lord thy God with all thy heart,' refers to the present. But how can we comply with this requirement so long as sin is in our heart? Our love is defective just in proportion as sin remains in us. All God's commands imply the promise of ability to obey. This command, therefore, must mean that God purposes to cleanse our hearts from all sin now, or He would require an impossibility—a charge which few would dare to make. This conclusion is inevitable. 'The blood of Jesus *cleanseth*.' How we glory in proclaiming this present tense of grace!

"But some cannot understand how this cleansing is through the blood of Jesus. We need to explain, perhaps, that we are obliged in this, as in other cases, to use figurative language. We sing of the 'fountain filled with blood;' but we all know there is no such fountain. When we speak of the blood of Jesus cleansing from sin, we do not mean that the blood of

Christ is literally applied to the heart. What is meant is, that through His great atoning work Christ has procured, or purchased, complete deliverance from sin for us, exactly as He has made forgiveness possible to us.

"But whilst Christ is thus through His death what may be termed the *procuring cause* of sanctification, the work itself is wrought in us through the agency of the Holy Spirit. All inward renewal is the result of His operation; He is the administrator of the covenant of grace, the 'executive of the Godhead.' He comes to the heart in sanctifying power, excluding the evil and filling it with love (when we believe the blood cleanseth us from all sin), just as He comes in regenerating power when we believe for forgiveness and are adopted into the family of God.

"The blood is the price of redemption. Through it Christ procures for us the gift of the Holy Ghost, and when He fills the heart, His presence excludes all sin as light excludes darkness. But for the shedding of the blood of Christ the Holy Ghost would never have been given. So it is the Cross at the beginning, and the Cross all the way through.

"This is the teaching of the writer of the Epistle to the Hebrews: 'By the which will, we are sanctified through the offering of the body of Jesus (Christ) once for all.' Some believe we are justified by faith, and sanctified by works. This passage teaches that it is God's will that we should be sanctified exactly as we are justified, 'through the offering of the body of Jesus Christ,' or through the shedding of the blood of Christ, 'once for all.' Provision for our sanctification has been made as fully as for our justification, and faith must receive it. Suppose I went to some jeweller's shop, and purchased a beautiful timepiece for a friend, I leave my card with the jeweller, saying, 'I have bought this for a friend; when he presents a card like this, please let him have it.' I go to my friend and tell him what I have done, and give him a card similar to the one I have left with the jeweller. Now, to whom does that timepiece belong? Not to the jeweller, I have paid him for it; not to myself, I have bought it for my friend. It belongs to him. But he will never have it unless he presents the card I gave him and claims it. In like manner full salvation has been purchased for us; but many Christians do not realise it. Why? Because they have not claimed their heritage. Jesus Christ is to no man practically any more than what He is to that man's faith. In other words, He is our Saviour just so far as we trust Him to save us. If we are not saved from all sin the fault is our own. A perfect Saviour and a perfect salvation must always go together. Would that to every believer's apprehension Christ was 'Almighty to save' here and now!

"We might argue that full salvation is immediately attainable, because all the commands and promises imply present blessing; or because it is received by faith, and faith cannot be otherwise than an instantaneous operation; or because universal testimony harmonises with this view. We might also mention scores of scriptures sustaining this teaching. But what more is needed than the passage we are considering? 'The blood of Jesus Christ, His Son, cleanseth us from all sin.' In the case of a direct utterance like this one single inspired declaration is competent to establish any truth. 'Repeated and varied statements,' it has been well said, 'may heighten the certainty that the exact idea has been apprehended, but one, "Thus saith the Lord," is sufficient to settle the most difficult proposition.' If there were no other scripture to be found which teaches the present possibility of deliverance from all sin, this is enough.

It was under the Holy Spirit's illumination of this very verse that the writer for the first time saw, and was enabled to claim, his privilege in this matter. His heart thrills now at the remembrance of that day when he joyously exclaimed, 'I see it all; the blessing is mine, "the blood cleanseth;"' and there and then the work was done.

"Blessed word, 'cleanseth'! What a door of hope and joy this word has opened to many! Does it not teach, as some writer puts it, 'a continual present, always a present tense, not a present which the next moment becomes a past; it goes on cleansing; not a coming to be cleansed in the fountain only, but a remaining in the fountain.' What better interpretation will it bear than that, as life is made up of one continual now, 'Jesus saves all the time' by saving every *now?* It is ever present provision for ever-present need, Christ always a present Saviour. To contend, as some do, that after full salvation is once received, the blood of Jesus Christ is no longer continuously needed, is as absurd as to maintain that because it is noonday the sun is not needed. As we have already stated, the heart is only cleansed by the Holy Spirit taking full possession, and it is only kept clean by His remaining. He is retained by the same continuous acting of faith by which we first received Him. We preach, therefore, a moment by moment salvation, maintained by a perpetual faith in the cleansing blood.

"What difficulties would be removed if it were everywhere emphasised that by full salvation is meant, not some immutable state which is attained after a desperate venture of faith once for all, but rather a *maintained condition*, which is ours so long as we live up to present light, and continue to trust the blood to cleanse us from all present defilement. Understanding this, should communion with God ever be broken, as it will be if there is even a momentary hesitation about yielding, obeying, or trusting? This need not continue three minutes; faith instantly plunges into the 'fountain open for sin and uncleanness,' and realises again its power to cleanse and restore.

"Faith in the spiritual world has been compared to breathing in the physical. We breathe this moment and receive the oxygen into our lungs; it purifies the blood which goes coursing through the system, carrying life and nutriment to all the tissues; but when another moment comes, we must breathe again; another moment again, and so on. Life is made up of successive acts of breathing. We breathe moment by moment, and live moment by moment. If we cease to breathe, we cease to live. In like manner we trust the blood of Jesus for cleansing this moment, and it cleanseth from all sin; another moment comes, and we trust again, and another moment again, and so on. We are thus kept clean exactly as we are made clean, through a constant succession of acts of faith in the cleansing blood. Blessed are those who have learned this secret. Present tense Christians all say that no words can describe the freedom and victory of such a life.

K

"But the question is often asked, 'Is it possible for a believer to pass instantly from childhood to manhood in Christian experience? Can we become full-grown in a day?' There can be but one answer to these inquiries, and that a negative one. The advocates of instantaneous and entire cleansing are careful to discriminate between purity of heart and maturity of Christian character. The entire cleansing received by faith is perfect health of soul, but it is not perfect development. It may not be generally known that the word 'health' and the word 'holy' come from the same root. Perfect health is the entire absence of disease; perfect holiness is the entire absence of sin. Christian purity brings finality to nothing but inbred sin. It is the field cleared of the noxious weeds, not the ripe, waving harvest. It is the best preparation for growth, not the consummation of growth. 'The heart may be cleansed from all sin,' says Bishop Hamline, 'while our graces are immature; and entire cleansing is the best preparation for their unembarrassed and rapid growth.' We must seek a clean heart first, and look for maturity in the order of Divine appointment. Purity is not the goal, but rather a new starting-point. In conversion all the graces of the Spirit are implanted in the soul: they are there in germ, but, of course, not developed. But so long as there are remains of the carnal mind within, not only are the graces of the Spirit there, but their opposites are there also, which are like weeds about the root of a plant impeding its growth. No grace of the Spirit can be helped in its development by the presence of its opposite. A little unbelief will be of no help to our faith; nor a little pride to our humility. Proclivities towards sin never yet helped a man into conformity to God. Sin in the heart makes us like a child that is sickly, or a tree with a worm at the root. Some hope by cultivating the graces of the Spirit to grow into purity, which is like a man cultivating the vegetables in his garden to grow the weeds out from about the roots of the plants. Common sense says, 'Pluck up the weeds, and give the plant a fair chance for growth and development.' This is the Divine method. God cleanses the heart from inbred sin, after which growth is always more rapid and symmetrical; advancement in knowledge and love of God and all spiritual excellence become possible then as they never were before. Maturity is the result of experience, trial, conflict, and requires time; but in purity we grasp by faith the sin-consuming power that sweeps the heart clean at a stroke. There may be preparations for it and approaches to it, but there is a moment when it is done. Believing now, we are pardoned now; believing now, we are cleansed from all sin now.

"But some cannot understand how it is possible to continue believing every moment in this way. Will not business and other matters take the attention away? We are not always thinking about breathing, and yet we always are breathing. 'But,' they say, 'it is natural for me to breathe.' It may become such a habit of soul to believe that we shall do it just as we breathe without thinking about it. The difficulty is all at first. It requires, then, the effort of the will, but by and by, through the constant repetition of the act it becomes almost as natural to believe as to breathe. Believing becomes so thoroughly the attitude of the soul that the mind is like the pointer of a compass. You may take it and bring it from the north to the south, east, or west, and as long as your finger is upon it, it will remain there; but remove the finger, and it will soon fly back again to the north. So it is with those who have cultivated this habit of faith. The mind returns again to this point, thought reverts to it naturally: it is the returning point of the soul—'The blood cleanseth from all sin.'

"But we must do something more than theorise on this subject. God wants witnesses. We might advertise a remedy for cancer, but who would believe in it, unless we could point to some we had cured? The testimony of the cleansed leper will do more to recommend the physician than the most persuasive and cogent arguments. Three times St. Paul had his commission renewed, which was not so much to preach as to testify. St. John recognises testimony as one of the chief elements of evangelical power; hence the frequent occurrence of the words 'We know,' so characteristic of his Epistles. He believed men might be saved from all sin, and *know* it, so as to be able to testify as he did, 'The blood of Jesus cleanseth *us* from all sin.' If all our pulpits were converted from the advocate's stand to a witness-box, what a stir it would make next Sunday. The great want of the times is a witnessing Church and ministry. 'Ye are my witnesses,' saith the Lord. Not that we would recommend loud professions as to attainments. Instead of professing anything, let us confess Christ as a Saviour from all sin, if we have proved Him to be such. This will make Him, and what He is to us, prominent, as contrasted with some attainment which might call attention to ourselves. Thousands of those who now clearly enjoy the experience of full salvation, acknowledge that it was through listening to the testimonies of credible witnesses to the power of Christ to save to the uttermost that they were first encouraged to believe in the possibility of such an experience, and stimulated to seek it. There is no more hopeful indication of the times than the fact that in all the Churches witnesses are being multiplied, who testify constantly, 'The blood of Jesus cleanseth *me* from all sin.' The Rev. John Fletcher once said to Mrs. Hester Ann Rogers—'Come, my sister, we will covenant together to spread the sacred flame, and testify before men and angels, "The blood of Jesus Christ cleanseth us from all sin."' With flowing tears Mrs. Rogers replied—'In the strength of Jesus I will!' and she did, until she went 'sweeping through the gates, washed in the blood of the Lamb.' If all our people would join us in a similar covenant, what an impression it would make upon the unbelieving world!

"When Bengel, the great scholar and commentator, was upon his death-bed, he requested one of his attendants to read out of the Scriptures. He read until he came to the passage—'The blood of Jesus Christ, His Son, cleanseth us from all sin.' 'Stop,' said the dying man, 'add no more, it is enough. Let me die on these words.'

"But if it be well to die on these words, it must surely be well to live on them. Some of us are doing it, and all our utterances fail to express the precious daily manifestations of Christ we have, as we realise Him to be a perfect Saviour. Space would fail to tell of all the blessedness and power this experience has brought. Let it suffice to say it marks always a crisis in the religious life of those who receive it.

It is an experience as much above the ordinary Christian experience as the ordinary Christian experience is above that of the worldling. Payson thus describes what it brought to him: 'The Sun of Righteousness gradually approached, appearing larger and brighter as He approached, until His brightness filled the whole hemisphere, pouring forth a flood of light and glory, in which I seemed to float like an insect in the beams of the sun, exulting yet almost trembling, and wondering with unutterable wonder why God should deign thus to shine upon such a sinful worm.'

"Some say they are hungering and thirsting for this experience, but they cannot believe. Such need to be reminded that God's commands are 'enablings.' There is always a moral cause of unbelief, '*If we walk in the light, the blood cleanseth,*' but only those who live up to present light can believe the promise. This is the reason why many fail.

"A lady once came to the writer and said, 'I do so want to be cleansed, but I cannot believe the blood cleanseth *me* from all sin.' 'Are you walking in the light?' 'So far as I know the will of God,' she replied, 'I am doing it, and I have made up my mind to do it whatever it costs.' 'This is walking in the light. We are only responsible for what we know, and if you are doing the will of God as far as you know it, and are determined to do it as far as it is revealed to you, you fulfil the condition. Now believe the promise, "The blood of Jesus cleanseth you from all sin."' 'Oh,' she said, 'I cannot do that.' So we put the truth before her as follows: 'You remember that nobleman who came to Jesus on behalf of his son?' 'Yes.' 'What did Jesus say? "Go thy way, thy son liveth!"' 'Yes.' 'And what did he do? He went his way, believing the word that Jesus had spoken!' 'Yes.' 'Now, suppose that nobleman had met a friend a few minutes afterwards, and had told him his son was better, would he have done right or wrong? Mark, the servants had not yet met him, nor had he been home to see, and yet he says, "My son is better."' 'He would have done right,' she said, 'because he had the word of Jesus for it, and was not that enough?' 'Exactly,' the writer replied. 'And have not you the word of Jesus that the blood cleanseth from all sin?' She saw it, and hesitated but a moment. 'If that nobleman could believe the word of God, I can; I will believe the blood cleanseth *me* from all sin.' She went home believing. Two or three days afterwards the writer met her again. She came to him with a beaming face, and, extending her hand, said, 'Oh, do help me to praise God! I had hardly left you the other day before the servants met me, and said, "It is all right;" and I have had the blessed assurance ever since.'

"If all our readers would cast themselves upon God's immutable promise in like manner, they too would receive the witness of cleansing, and help to augment the number of the joyful multitude who have covenanted everywhere to testify, as opportunity serves, 'The blood of Jesus Christ, His Son, cleanseth *us* from all sin.'

> "'Saviour, to Thee my soul looks up,
> My present Saviour Thou;
> In all the confidence of hope
> I claim the blessing now.'"

After he has explained this doctrine, it has been usual with Mr. Cook to invite Christians to come forward and seek it, much in the same way as penitents are directed to seek justification. How many Christians have entered into "the Sabbath of God's love" during these mission services it would be impossible to say, but many letters are before me, written by ministers and people, by men and women, by old and by young, bearing testimony to the precious blessings which the writers have received on these occasions, and describing the results that have followed in their experience and in their work for Christ.

A Lancashire class-leader writes, under date April 2nd, 1888: "I must for ever thank you for enabling me to believe for full salvation. It makes me feel ashamed of myself, that for more than thirty years I have been professing to love God, and yet did not dare to trust His Word. Now, thank God, I know something of the perfect love which casts out fear. At first the brightness of my life was, I thought, too good to last, and I often wondered how it would be when a big trouble came. Well, I cannot express to you how wonderfully the precious promises have been fulfilled in me. Well might the apostle say, 'Above all we can ask or think.' I am constantly urging the importance of full salvation on my members, and, I hope, with good results." Among many Wesleyan ministers who have written to acknowledge the blessing they have received at the holiness-meetings conducted by our Evangelist, is one who has himself been much blessed in leading others into the Canaan of perfect love, and who expresses much gratitude to God, as well as many thanks to His servant, for help thus given. Several clergymen have also acknowledged that this Methodist preacher has been used by God to teach them what they did not know of the privileges of believers. One of these has taken a prominent part in evangelistic work, and has used the light he received through the teaching of Mr. Cook to great advantage.

Many testimonies have been published in the *King's Highway* by persons who have felt it their duty to witness to full salvation, and who were led into the deeper things of God by Mr. Cook. But of these we cannot speak particularly.

The late Rev. Herbert Hoare is now with God; let him, though dead, bear his testimony to the effect produced upon the Church by the teaching of this blessed truth. He wrote, under date February 14th, 1884, and his letter refers to the great Sheffield mission. These are his words: "One of the most welcome results of the mission is the quickening of the spiritual life of our people. It is delightful to listen to their experience. It is so different now, and so superior. The two services for the promotion of holiness you held, on the Wednesday and Thursday afternoons, have already brought forth much fruit, so many in the families of our people having had their Christian life enlarged and strengthened. Never, I think, has a blessing been vouchsafed on so large a scale to our Sheffield Methodism as during our never-to-be-forgotten mission."

When Mr. Cook was preaching in Cambridge, he was asked by a number of undergraduates to meet them privately for conversation and prayer on the subject of entire sanctification. He accordingly did so, and a most impressive service was held. The presence of God was so powerfully felt, that preacher and hearers—all young men alike—were not conscious of anything else. On that memorable occasion God took possession of the hearts of some of those scholars, who from that day began to live a brighter and more useful Christian life. Who can tell what the indirect result of such a meeting of educated young men may be! Some who were then present are now filling important positions in the Church of England and in other Churches, and it may be, they will continue to spread the truth they then embraced to the end of life. At the seat of the sister University, Mr. Cook held a similar meeting. In the Oxford Wesleyan Chapel he had the joy to see a dozen University men kneeling at the communion rail and seeking purity of heart. The result was, that the news of this teaching and movement spread amongst the undergraduates, and a desire was expressed by some who scrupled to enter the Wesleyan Chapel, to know more of what appeared to them to be a new doctrine. The Mayor of Oxford courteously placed the Council Chamber at the Evangelist's disposal, and in that municipal building he met a number of Oxford students and told them all that was in his heart. By arrangement with some friendly students, Mr. Cook met a number of Oxford men in the very room in which it is supposed that the "Holy Club" used to meet; and he instructed them from the Holy Scriptures in the nature of this priceless blessing. It is impossible not to think of Mr. Wesley in this connection. If he could have foreseen, in his early days at Oxford, that a century after his decease one of his preachers would be closeted with a number of students attached to the University which he loved so much, and would be leading them into the possession of full salvation, he would have rejoiced in spirit. Only a few months before his death Mr. Wesley wrote: "This doctrine [of full sanctification] is the grand *depositum* which God has lodged with the people called Methodists; and, for the sake of propagating this chiefly, He appears to have raised them up." It would therefore have been pleasing to Wesley had he known that, through the instrumentality of one of his preachers, God would, towards the end of the nineteenth century, raise up in Cambridge and Oxford Universities witnesses of this glorious truth. The two classes of our population most alienated from the Christian Church to-day are the scholars and the artisans. In a subsequent chapter it will appear that God has graciously used Mr. Cook to win to Christ multitudes of the latter class, and this chapter is intended in part to show that even among the former class his labours have not been without fruit. A number of undergraduates cross-examined Mr. Cook on one of the occasions just referred to, concerning his own experience. They asked him many questions, not in a captious, but in a truth-seeking spirit, as to the way in which God had led him, and the power God had given him over sin. He answered their inquiries with perfect frankness, for

"What we have felt and seen,
With confidence we tell,"

both to scholars and to artisans. As the result of this interview, the young men confessed to Mr. Cook, that although his teaching was to them strange and beyond *their* experience, they believed that it was in accord with his own experience.

A minister writes: "I desire with others to testify of the grace of God. During the mission services I have afresh consecrated myself to God, and richly experienced Christ in me, the hope of glory. What a wonderful sense of light and love fills our hearts when we give up *trying* to believe, and simply trust and obey. Although I have known much of God's sanctifying grace, yet I shall always thank God for the clearer light and greater blessing I have received during your mission."

An active Christian worker, known to the writer, sends the news of much blessing received by him at one of the holiness-meetings which Mr. Cock addressed. He testifies that during the delivery of the address he was enabled to claim the fulfilment of the text, " The blood of Jesus Christ, His Son, cleanseth us from all sin ;" and he adds that he did not stand up, or go forward as a seeker after holiness, when others did, because, having found the blessing in his pew, it seemed to him that to do so would be to cast doubt upon the work which God had wrought within his soul.

During the last seven years a convention has been held annually in Southport for the purpose of spreading this blessing. The Rev. W H. Tindall was the prime mover in this new advance, and it has been Mr. Cook's privilege to be associated with Mr. Tindall in the conduct of this movement from the first. In some respects these Southport conventions have been similar to the well-known Keswick conventions. The services have extended over the week, and have been largely attended by persons belonging to different Churches, who have come from many parts of the United Kingdom, and even from abroad. Many ministers have taken part in the conventions ; the teaching has been scriptural, and therefore in accord with the standard works of Methodism ; and the blessing of God has rested upon the services every year in a marked manner. The addresses given on these occasions have also been reported in several organs of the press, and thus the great subject has been brought before the Connexion, with what results the day will declare.

For any Methodist to make light of this doctrine is for such an one to prove himself unworthy of that "glorious ancestry" on which all Methodists are wont to "enlarge," and by enlarging upon which they

"Produce their debt instead of their discharge."

For any Methodist preacher to do this, is for him to prove that, whatever his graces and gifts may be, his place is not in the Wesleyan-Methodist ministry. At least, so John Wesley thought within three or four months of his decease. Writing to Adam Clarke in November 1790, Mr. Wesley says: "If we can prove that any of our local preachers or leaders, either directly or indirectly, speak against (perfect love), let him be a local preacher or leader no longer. I doubt whether he should continue in Society. Because he that could speak thus in our congregations cannot be an honest man."

We are not concerned to defend all the expressions that are used by various speakers to set forth this indescribable blessing, but when certain words are quoted from the Rev. Dr. Pope's *Compendium of Theology*, we feel it incumbent upon us to make a rejoinder.

In that great work Dr Pope has said: "Never do we read of a Higher Life that is other than the intensification of the lower; never of a Second Blessing that is more than the unrestrained outpouring of the same Spirit who gave the first" (vol. iii. p. 44). But in my own hearing, at a holiness convention held in Bradford shortly before Mr. Cook entered upon his work in that district, Dr. Pope recanted these words, and declared that he stood as "a penitent" for having written them. On another occasion, when he was addressing a large number of his brethren, Dr. Pope said: "I have sometimes delicately scrupled at this, that, and the other expression, and I have wondered whether it is right to speak of a 'second blessing.' But I have read the text in which our Saviour takes a blind man and partially restores his sight, and then, holding the man up before us for a little while that we may study his state, which is a great advance upon what it was, He lets us watch the struggle. He touched him again, and he saw every man clearly. In the face of that narrative, and in the face of the experience of multitudes of our fathers, and of the testimonies of multitudes now living, and in the face of the deep instinct of my own unworthy heart, I will never again write against the phraseology to which I have referred."

Thomas Cook would wish to say with Thomas Collins: "Among the brotherhood I am but a child; yet it seems to me I could whisper in the ears of greater men a more excellent way. Wesley tells it, the Bible tells it. Let every Methodist preacher get, keep, and preach full salvation, and God will then put His own seal upon His sanctifying Word."

"Give me," said Wesley, "one hundred preachers who fear nothing but sin, and desire nothing but God, and I care not a straw whether they be clergymen or laymen; such alone will shake the gates of hell, and set up the kingdom of heaven upon earth."

May God ever give such preachers to Methodism, and then, as sure as night follows day, the design of God in raising up Methodism will be answered, and the nation will be reformed, and scriptural holiness will be spread over the land.

CHAPTER VIII.

MEN'S MEETINGS.

THERE have been few periods in the history of our country when there has been more occasion for anxiety about the future of England than there is at the present time. For weal or for woe the destinies of the British Empire are now entrusted to the masses of the people. We have "shot Niagara," and Carlyle's question, "What after?" may well ring in the ears of thoughtful patriots. How will the industrial classes meet their great responsibilities? Will they only pay regard to what they consider to be their own interests, and vote solidly for class legislation? The newspapers are full of what they call "The Labour Movement," and whereunto this movement will grow no man knows. Only recently a Labour Congress has been held in Brussels, to which as many as sixty newspaper reporters were sent, and the proceedings of which were recorded in all the principal papers of Europe and the United States of America. What are "our masters" bent upon doing? When labour is united in one solid phalanx, as it bids fair to be before the world is much older, what will be the effect of this "new unionism"? The present writer, at all events, has no fear of a sober and

Christian democracy, but he has grave fears for any country which is governed by an atheistic or immoral democracy.

It is impossible not to feel much sympathy with the aspirations of the artisan class. So far are we from sharing the feelings of those comfortable classes who would fain quench these aspirations, and who lift up their hands in horror when they hear them expounded by Labour representatives, and exclaim: "Good heavens, what will become of *us* if all these claims are conceded?"—so far are we from sharing such sentiments, that we are distinctly in accord with the Rev. J. M. Wilson, M.A., late of Clifton College, who has said that if all the members of the Christian Churches were to be filled with the Spirit of Christ, they would instantly bend their energies to the task of promoting the social and moral improvement of the working classes.

Out of every ten inhabitants of the British Isles only three live in comfort, the other seven are scarcely above the line of poverty. In London alone there is much reason to believe that one in every four adults dies dependent on public charity. That estimate does not include those in receipt of out-door relief. It is an estimate which includes all classes. The proportion amongst the working classes *alone* must be higher. An official return, made in 1889, gives over 51,000 children in the elementary day schools in London who habitually attend in want of food. Speaking of these semi-starved children, Mr. Charles Booth says, in his great work on *Life and Labour in London:* "Puny, pale-faced, scantily clad, and badly shod, these small and feeble folk may be found sitting limp and chill on the school benches in all the poorer parts of London."

It is unworthy of any man to say that the poverty of the very poor is self-inflicted, and that therefore it does not concern him. That much of the destitution which appals us *is* self-inflicted, is no doubt true, but that does not lessen the difficulty of the problem which now confronts us. It must also be remembered that the struggle for existence is keener than it ever was. Men over forty years of age find it difficult to get employment if once they are out of work, and many thousands who have worked hard and not been unthrifty in their habits, but who have been burdened with large families, are utterly unable to provide for old age, and have no prospect before them but that of the workhouse. More than half our paupers are over sixty-five years of age. *One* person in every *three* of all classes attaining to old age in this country is dependent for subsistence on parish relief, given either within or without the walls of the workhouse.

Nor is it correct to say that the purchasing power of money is greater than it was formerly. In the case of rich men this is so. It is not so in the case of others. Bread is happily much cheaper, and so are clothes, but rent has increased during the last fifty years a hundred and fifty per cent. The writer recently met a godly Methodist labourer in London, who, when he works a full week, and is not hindered an hour by the rain, earns twenty-four shillings and sixpence in six days, out of which he pays as much as eight shillings and sixpence a week for rent. Vegetables, milk, eggs, butter, cheese, coals, and meat are all dearer than they used to be, and consequently the difficulty of bringing up a large family on a small and precarious income is greater than it was in "the good old times." All over England are families living in single rooms, so that it is impossible for the sexes to be brought up separately; and what the effect of bringing them up together must be, especially when, as too often happens, the parents themselves are not of pure habits, the reader may imagine. Capital and labour are constantly warring against each other, and social peace appears to be a remote prospect.

It does not become any one of us, therefore, to be "at ease in Zion," but all of us should seek to improve the condition of the people, and to effect a material as well as moral reformation in this well-favoured country.

I have felt it right to make these statements in order that they may balance what is about to follow.

Mr. Cook has not played the *rôle* of social reformer or Christian socialist, whatever that phrase may mean. With a singleness of purpose which must satisfy Mr. Spurgeon himself, he has prosecuted his one work, and continued to be a man of one idea. He has fought neither with great nor small, save only with human sin; and although the writer has not followed his example, and restricted his efforts to the promotion of the spiritual interests of the people, he fully believes that Mr. Cook has been well advised in the course he has taken. God has given our Evangelist a *special* work to do, and he has neither time nor strength to undertake additional tasks. As he has "opportunity" he does "good unto all men," but he has not the "opportunity" which some others have of doing *various* kinds of good. It is of the utmost importance that Christian men should not be inactive in promoting social reform, as they are sometimes charged, by socialists, with being. It is also most desirable that such movements as those which are designed to promote the wholesome housing of the poor, to destroy the evils of the sweating system, to reduce to reasonable limits the working hours of the sons of toil, to reconcile capital and labour, to further industrial co-operation, to reform the drinking habits of the masses of the people, to inculcate habits of thrift, and to prepare the way for a system of national insurance which shall secure to industrious men and women an honest and independent subsistence in old age, when they are no longer able to earn their bread by the sweat of their brow,—I say, it is most desirable that none of these ameliorative measures should be left to the advocacy of extreme outsiders, but should all be espoused and guided by the wisest and most high-minded Christian men and women whom the Churches possess. If the olive tree will leave its fatness and consent to reign over the trees, the services of the bramble may be dispensed with; but if the olive tree declines this responsibility, the bramble may be forced upon the trees by the necessity which all feel to have some king to reign over them. Nothing, therefore, that this chapter contains is intended to discourage either Christian ministers or laymen from taking their full share in every movement for the practical amelioration of the condition of our fellow-countrymen.

Mr. Cook has set his brethren an excellent example, inasmuch as during the last ten years he has attracted to the house of God many thousands of working men, and has preached the gospel to them, and, by the blessing of God, has secured the adhesion of large numbers of them to the cause of Christ. Probably it is pretty well known that neither the holiness-meetings, nor the young people's services, nor the inquiry-rooms, are a more regular feature of Mr. Cook's missions than are the men's meetings; but the precise object of these meetings, and the way in which they are conducted, may not be so widely known. It is only four or five years ago since we heard the late Rev. Dr. Osborn ask in Conference what the design was of these men's meetings. That venerable minister, always on the alert to discover any new advance in Methodism, and ever ready to be a discerner of spirits, expressed a slight fear lest these meetings should be so managed as to result in injury to the work of God. At the same time, he admitted that, under wise management, the men's meetings might further the gospel very largely. He therefore asked for information. As some who read these pages may even now be where that distinguished minister then was, this chapter may serve a useful purpose.

Usually on the second Sunday afternoon of the mission, and, when the mission extends over three Sundays, on the afternoon of the third Sunday also, it is Mr. Cook's custom to hold a service for men only.

During the previous week tickets advertising the service are freely distributed by the mission workers in the workshops and houses of the neighbourhood, the object of the ticket being, not to exclude any persons from the chapel who may apply for admission without a ticket, but to make the meeting known, and to invest it with additional interest. All fish are not caught in the same way. Trout, it is said, are caught by tickling. Certainly some men are caught by innocent guile and Christian courtesy, who would otherwise elude the preacher's vigilance. Ask a man to attend a service, and the probability is he will suppose you want him to do *you* a favour. Give him a ticket admitting him to the service, and it is just as likely he will think you are doing *him* a kindness.

As a rule the chapel is well filled at the men's meeting, sometimes crowded; and always is it seen that, if the meeting can be repeated on the third Sunday, the attendance is larger than on the first occasion. As we have already seen, some of the largest chapels in the Connexion have been crowded to the doors year after year, during the last ten years, on these impressive occasions. There is little reason for the exclusion of women and children except this: their exclusion makes the service a novelty, and thus excites curiosity. It also makes the men less shy of coming; and gives the Evangelist freedom to speak, if he is so led, a little more plainly about particular sins.

But, generally speaking, the address given does not refer to "questions of the day," but to questions of eternity; and little, if anything, is said which all the world might not hear, and be the better for hearing. Again, I must guard myself against being supposed to wish to disparage the endeavours which some of my brethren make to apply Christianity to the problems of the day. Having myself attempted to do this with my one talent, I am not disposed to censure myself for so doing; nor am I willing even to seem to censure my friend Mr Hughes, who has used his five talents in St. James' Hall on Sunday afternoons in this particular way. Let the reader ponder these weighty words which Dr. Dale uttered in his own pulpit in the presence of many Wesleyan ministers, on the occasion of the last Birmingham Conference, held in the year 1879: "As yet, however, the Evangelical Revival has done very little to give us a nobler and more Christian ideal of practical life. It has been very timid. It has shrunk from politics. It has regarded literature and art with a certain measure of distrust. In business, it has been content with attaching Divine sanctions to recognised virtues. We are living in a new world, and Evangelicals do not seem to have discovered it. The immense development of the manufacturing industries, the wider separation of classes in great towns (a separation produced by the increase of commercial wealth), the new relations which have grown up between the employers and the employed, the spread of popular education, the growth of a vast popular literature, the increased political power of the masses of the people, the gradual decay of the old aristocratic organization of society, and the advance, in many forms, of the spirit of democracy,—have urgently demanded fresh applications of the eternal ideas of the Christian faith to conduct. But Evangelical Christians have hardly touched the new ethical problems which have come with the new time."

But every man in his own order. To each man the Master gives *his* work,—*i.e.* his own work,—for the doing of which he and no one else is held responsible. To Thomas Cook has been given a work than which there is none nobler,—the work of a Prime Minister is not so important. He has been sent to open the eyes of sinners, and to turn them from the power of Satan unto God; and he has sedulously avoided the snare into which that man of old fell who was too busy to do his duty, and who said, "While thy servant was busy here and there, he was gone."

Give to every workman in England a comfortable dwelling-house, with a plot of garden ground attached to it; make all the streets wide, and have them well lit; let there be public halls, free libraries, baths, wash-houses, gymnasia and recreation grounds within easy reach of our dense populations; supply every town with beautiful parks, in which fountains should play all the year round, and bands of music delight the ear of the crowd on summer evenings; multiply your free schools, in which the children of the poorest may have the opportunity of securing an education which may fittingly lead to a University course; run workmen's trains from pleasant suburbs to industrial centres, and give each man a season-ticket to carry him to and from his daily task,—and all this would be as nothing compared with what you have done for men, in bringing them to God, in securing for them the forgiveness of sins, and an inheritance among them that are sanctified by faith in Christ.

And this service God has graciously enabled Mr. Cook to render, by means of these meetings, to large numbers of men, belonging to all classes and of all ages.

At the close of the address,—which, in truth, is always a sermon,—the Evangelist follows the same course as at the evening services. The men are invited to stand up, in proof that they are penitent, and that they desire the prayers of the congregation. They are then directed to the inquiry-room, where experienced Christian men meet them, and help them as best they are able. Their names and addresses are carefully taken, and arrangements are at once made for visiting them in their homes, with a view to induce them to join some Christian Church.

The effect of the men's meeting upon the subsequent services of the mission is seen in the greater number of bare heads that may be counted on every occasion.

At some of the men's meetings very many conversions have taken place,—as, for example, at Sheffield, where a hundred men came out as inquirers at two such services. The converts thus made are naturally eager to attend the remaining services, and they swell the congregations. In the enthusiasm of their first love, they are sure to bring some of their "mates" with them, and thereby the interest and usefulness of the mission are extended.

If the reader will pardon the Hibernianism of a paragraph appearing in this chapter concerning the other sex, it will be a convenience to be permitted to say here, that Mr. Cook has not neglected "the religious sex." Women's meetings have been regularly held on week-day afternoons, to which mothers have been encouraged to bring their little ones, seeing that in many cases they could not come without them. Sometimes an adjoining room has been turned into a nursery; and thither the babies have been sent, to be taken care of by young ladies out of the congregation, who have thus for once consented to become "nursing mothers" for the Church, and thereby to liberate the poor mothers to attend to their souls' salvation.

Something is gained by these efforts to reach the sexes separately, and to reach the young people apart. We cannot divide our congregations into "standards," as the day-school teacher divides his scholars; but we may improvise services for men, and for women, and for children, and for Christians (as in the holiness-meetings), and for the unsaved (as in the evening evangelistic services), and thus go on reforming the nation and spreading scriptural holiness over the land.

It is much to be wished that the ablest ministers in the Churches would address themselves to the task of evangelising the working men of England. The Rev. J. M. Wilson, M.A., justly observes, that " many good people think that all that is necessary " (to secure this object) " is to send ill-instructed curates and Scripture-readers and Bible-women among the artisans: you might as well send squibs to put out a conflagration."

Statesmen of the first rank—Cabinet Ministers and even Prime Ministers—deem it worth their while " to stump the country," because they wish to influence " our masters " in exercising the franchise with which the nation has entrusted them. Why should not ministers of religion of the first rank be as wise in their generation as are the children of this world in theirs? Working men have *souls* as well as votes; and overseers of souls are bound to be at least as earnest in seeking to catch souls as politicians are to catch votes. Principal Fairbairn set an example worthy of imitation when, a few years ago, he left more congenial fields of labour, and spent six successive Sunday evenings in lecturing to the working men of Bradford on " Religion and History "

Dr. Parker made a laudable effort in the same direction, when, more recently, he held a series of conferences with working men in London. Dr. Parker is impulsive, and not without the defects of his qualities. He abandoned his conferences before they had really done much, or perhaps any, good. But if, instead of arguing with working men,—which, in truth, is not the best service that can be done them,—Dr. Parker would give himself occasionally to the work of meeting the objections of working men to religion, by instructing them in the nature of religion,—if he would abandon apology and reasoned defences of Christianity, and just exhibit to congregations of working men the religion of our Lord Jesus Christ in its truth and in its power,—there is no man living better qualified than he to secure our sons of industry for that Church which was founded by One who laboured with His hands as a carpenter, and whom the common people gladly heard.

The working men's meeting, which has now become a regular Conference service, is a step in the right direction, as also is the similar gathering held annually in connection with the Church Congress, and which is usually addressed by the finest speakers belonging to the Established Church.

During ten years Mr. Cook has been putting forth strenuous efforts to save the working men of England, and the following incident among many will serve to show that he has received wages and gathered fruit unto life eternal in this field also.

At the close of the Pendleton mission a service was held for the converts, seven hundred of whom were present. Moving about amongst them, Mr. Cook's attention was attracted by a woman who appeared to him to have seen a good deal of trouble. Her face, however, was lit up with a light as from heaven, and thus the Evangelist was led to ask if she had been blessed in the mission. Thereupon she told the Evangelist the following story, which will remind the Methodist reader of "Tom O'Jack's Lad," and of what he suffered in drowning a favourite dog which had been a snare and a besetment to him. The good woman said: "Aye, Mr. Cook, this has been a strange week in our house. My old man came to the men's meeting on Sunday afternoon. I don't know that he had been to a place of worship since we were married. When the service was over, he came home, and for a while was very quiet. Then he went into the yard and stayed there so long, that I was frightened, and I went to see what he was doing. I saw a strange sight. He had taken all the pigeons out of the cote and had wrung their necks, and there they were, lying in a row, fifteen of them, all dead, and he was crying over them. I said, 'Whatever are you doing, man?' He didn't answer me, but by and by he said, 'Get ready, lass, and go with me to chapel to-night.' I couldn't say anything, for I felt like crying mysen' He had never asked me to go to chapel with him before, and yet both of us had had a good bringing up. We were very quiet that day at tea; neither of us ate much; and we were at chapel in good time. When you had finished your sermon, and you asked those who wished to be saved to stand up, my husband was one of the first to rise, and I stood up too. Then we went into the inquiry-room, where we found peace with God." Pointing to a younger woman who sat next to her, the speaker added, "This is my daughter. She's been saved too, and her husband, and now we are all on the way to heaven, and we do thank God for this mission; the change in our home is wonderful."

CHAPTER IX.

SEALS OF APOSTLESHIP.

IT has pleased God to give Mr. Cook hundreds of converts to whom he can say, "Though ye have ten thousand tutors in Christ, yet have ye but one father; for in Jesus Christ have I begotten you through the gospel." The preceding chapters afford evidence that "the signs of an apostle" have been "wrought among" us "in all patience, in signs, and wonders, and mighty deeds." If Mr. Cook "be not an apostle unto others, yet doubtless" he is to those of whom this chapter treats, "for the seal of his apostleship" are they "in the Lord."

I wish to avoid giving undue publicity to circumstances of a sacred and confidential kind, which the persons chiefly concerned would prefer not to have published on the house-top. But as conversions are always interesting, and as they are the best credentials of the gospel; and as the record of them puts to silence the ignorance of foolish men, and at the same time encourages the Lord's children to expect continual displays of saving power,—it is hoped that something may be written about those who will be the crown of the Evangelist's rejoicing in the day of the Lord Jesus, without any offence being given or any harm being done.

A railway man, who reminds us of Mr. Cook's devoted Sunday-school teacher, writes to say that for twenty-five years he had never bowed his knees in prayer; but having been "brought to the Lord" at one of the mission services, he begs for prayer on behalf of his wife, who for ten years had been patient with a drunken, cruel husband, and who then needed to be saved, as he by God's mercy had been.

At one of the missions a lady attended who was in much mental trouble. Some of her ancestors had been of vicious habits; and although she had not contracted the same habits herself, she was much distressed by a theory which she had adopted, to the effect that vice is hereditary, and that the power of inherited vicious tendencies is so strong as in many cases to present an insuperable barrier to Divine grace. Writing, as I am, shortly after the close of the meetings of the British Association, held in Cardiff in August 1891, I am reminded of an address given on that occasion on "Instinctive Criminality," the gist of which is found in the following passage which I cull from the report in the *Times* newspaper: "Instinctive criminality follows the same lines as regards mode of transmission as do most other diseased conditions. The instinctive criminal is on all-fours with the idiot, the epileptic, the suicide, and the insane, and is equally to be pitied and humanely treated. He is, in fact, as much sinned against as sinning." So this lady thought. She also found a great stumbling-block to faith in God in the passage found in 1 Kings xxii. 20–23, as, indeed, have others who have not fully learnt how to read the Old Testament. But after a long struggle she writes: "I have fought hard, and have found that Jesus is mighty to save. All doubts are gone, and I can say with my whole heart that I believe that Jesus died for *me*, and has redeemed me with His precious blood. Since I have trusted I have been so happy, and I would not part with the evidence my Saviour has given me for all the world's wealth. Will you believe that the miserable, doubting creature you saw at —— is now going to testify to all of the saving power of Jesus?"

The difficulty of this inquirer concerning heredity is no small one, and it is one which raises a question that must receive greater attention in the future than it has done in the past. A sober-minded and most devout Christian writer has said that it is possible that he himself finds it harder to-day to live a pure and good life than he otherwise would do, because some ancestor of his in the days of King John lived an impure and vicious life. Apart from all rhetorical exaggeration, there is much truth in the remark, and it seems necessary that the attention, not only of parents, but of potential parents, should be directed to this question. Young people should be cautioned by proper persons— and who so proper as their own fathers and mothers?— to remember this consideration in offering and accepting love, lest their posterity should have the sins of their fathers visited upon them in one of the direst of all ways. And men and women should be entreated to live purely and soberly, in order that they may not transmit to their children vicious tendencies from which the grace of God may *scarcely* be able to extricate them.

God be praised, however, that "instinctive" vice may be subdued, for "with God all things are possible." The writer himself has met with a beautiful Christian, now with God, whose father, according to the evidence of his own wife, was never known to go to bed sober for fourteen years. But such conversions are as rare as that of the penitent thief, which, as the old divines used to say with perfect truth, is given as a *solitary* instance, that while none may despair of the grace of God, none may presume to postpone repentance until the eleventh hour.

Another friend writes : " How many hearts are full of gratitude to you for leading them to Jesus, but none is so full as mine. Your sermon on Sunday night did not impress me much, but afterwards when you were praying I felt a great pain come into my heart all at once, and it got worse and worse until I could bear it no longer. Then when you came and talked to me, it grew less and less. When I get to heaven, my chief delight and joy, next to seeing Jesus, will be to see you."

A husband and a wife write from the beautiful Channel Islands to tell of their newly-found peace, and they report the conversion of a friend also, the results of the same mission. A father sends a sovereign from Sheffield as a thank-offering for the conversion of a son who had become a source of anxiety, but had been blessed through Mr. Cook's ministry A Dublin correspondent writes to say that he was a Roman Catholic, but through curiosity he went to Mr. Cook's Dublin mission, and was converted. His relatives have " turned completely against him," and he begs for the prayers of the Evangelist.

Sometimes when we think that the Lord came to send peace on earth, we find that He came to bring a sword, and that a man's enemies are they of his own household. Among many ministers who write to this young Evangelist to acknowledge the blessing God has given them by his instrumentality, is one who says: "Although I had known much of God's sanctifying grace, I shall always thank God for the clearer light and greater blessing that I received during your services." A Plymouth correspondent sends word that his wife had received a great blessing at Mr. Cook's mission, and had confessed it before him and the maid-servant, with the result that the maid was earnestly seeking a like blessing. He writes on a Sunday, and adds: "No hot dinner to-day, Hallelujah!" And he subjoins a postscript: "In haste to the open-air service."

A poor steward, or, to use plainer language, a church officer, whose duty it is to relieve the poor out of funds provided for that purpose, writes: "I am thankful to say that after leaving you yesterday I was able to fully surrender myself to Christ." All stewards are supposed to be Christian men. They are entrusted with sacred functions, for they are members of the leaders' meeting, which is composed in the main of sub-pastors of the Church, and has charge of the *souls* of the members of the Church. But, alas! the supposition is not always well founded, and stewards are sometimes met with who do not enjoy a personal, conscious, happy salvation, as every Methodist ought to do.

This sincere steward said to Mr. Cook in an after-meeting: "If I were to become a Christian in the sense in which you use the word, it would involve a revolution in my business." He afterwards explained that he was a builder, and he described some of the tricks, *i.e.* sins, of that particular trade. The Evangelist told him that it was not necessary for him to live, but it was necessary to save his soul, which he could not do if he continued to defraud his neighbour. He exhorted him to consider the matter well before he decided to reject Christ for the sake of pelf. The penitent man promised to do so, and went his way. The result is told in the words already cited. He is now a consistent and useful officer of the church, and, moreover, a class-leader. The superintendent minister of one of our largest Circuits, in which Mr. Cook held a mission, writes to tell of a Roman Catholic woman who was saved at one of the mission services, and who took a ticket for the men's meeting for her husband. The husband had taken an oath twenty-three years before that he would never enter a Protestant place of worship; but when his wife brought him this ticket he considered he was liberated from his promise, and he went, and found salvation. The priest called to see his stray sheep, but the woman bade him come no more; for, said she, with charming simplicity, "When I came to confess to you, I didn't know the Lord would hear *me*." How many thousands of Roman Catholics are there—especially on the Continent—who do not know that the Lord will hear *them*, and who ignorantly worship God through the mediation of their priests! The minister adds: "God bless you, dear fellow, you have helped me very much. My work here has been harder than anything I have ever known. But we shall triumph."

It has been the joy of Mr. Cook to lead to Christ all

sorts of people. Many boys and girls, as we shall soon see, are among his most precious converts. Aged people, young men and young women, poor abandoned characters, respectable seat-holders, and persons of culture have received the word of truth from his lips, and been made partakers of a common salvation. The late Mr. J. Beauchamp writes, under date March the 18th, 1889, a touching letter, all the more pathetic now, because he has joined the lamented son of whom he speaks. He says: "You may perhaps have noticed in the *Recorder* an account of our son Godfrey, who died, after a very few days' illness, in his rooms in St. John's College, Cambridge, and who was a young man of very great promise. It will gratify you to know that when you conducted services in Cambridge he was led by your addresses to give his heart to God. He became a member of Society, and lived a very pure and beautiful life. High hopes were entertained of his success in the University by Dr. Moulton and his friends at the Leys School; but, taking cold, he was cut off before his twentieth year. On the first Sunday of the year he united in the Covenant service with his mother and myself. We cannot be too thankful to you for the blessed influence which, under God, you were enabled to exercise over his short but not useless life." The Rev. Dr. Moulton interred this young convert, and on the Sunday following the interment Archdeacon Farrar referred to his death in the University Church in affecting terms. Blessed be God for so many sheaves as are safely gathered in God's garner!

An Oldham convert writes to express thankfulness, and adds, "I shudder to think what I might have been, if it had not been for your mission."

It has pleased God to make Mr. Cook very useful to large numbers of ministers' children. The wife of a Wesleyan superintendent, herself the daughter of a distinguished ex-president, told the writer a short time since, with much feeling, that Mr. Cook had been very much blessed to her children, and many other ministers' wives may say the same. Here is a touching record likely to make the water stand in the eyes of any preacher who has sons of his own. It was written by the son of a minister who was elected for the first time at the Nottingham Conference as Chairman of a District, on the fly-leaf of the youth's Bible: " I gave my heart to God this day, January 17th, 1886."

Three workmen send a joint-letter from one of Her Majesty's dockyards, to inform the Evangelist of the good which one of their fellow-workmen had received at a men's meeting held during a mission. A young man writes to say that when he attended one of Mr. Cook's services at Tredegar, and saw Mr. Cook enter the pulpit, he said to himself: " If ever I get converted, it will not be under *that* man!" But he broke down at the close of the service, entered the inquiry-room, found peace with God, and, having laboured successfully as a lay evangelist, entered the ministry.

Upon one occasion Mr Cook went to conduct a mission in a remote part of the Connexion. He was, as sometimes happens, received as a guest by a gentleman whose wife deemed it wise, as a precautionary measure, to tell the Evangelist before he began his first service, that he (her husband) was not in sympathy with missions; neither was the daughter, who, having just returned from a Continental boarding-school, was not likely to look with favour upon movements of this kind. The Evangelist thereupon decided to take the matter to God in prayer, and to seek for Divine interposition. In the afternoon of the first Sunday, Mr. Cook, as his custom is, held a young people's service, and when he had concluded a brief address, he appealed for some volunteer who would come out and confess a determination to be the Lord's. Hardly had he made the appeal before he heard a movement behind him, and ere he had time to look round to see what was the cause of it, the daughter of his host stood by his side, in front of the congregation, and, with tears in her eyes, asked what she must do to be saved. She was directed to the inquiry-room, where she was soon made happy in the love of God.

In the evening of the same day, amongst the first to rise in answer to Mr. Cook's appeal was the gentleman himself, the Evangelist's host, who, soon after rising, walked down the aisle, in the presence of many of his workpeople, and avowed himself on the Lord's side hereafter. What the effect of these beautiful public conversions was may easily be imagined, as also may the useful service which this kind-hearted gentleman and educated young lady have since been enabled to render to Methodism in their own town.

Mr. Jabez Woolley has been the means of doing much good as an evangelist, in company with his friend Mr. Joshua Dawson; and it is pleasing to know that Mr. Cook has been used in effecting the conversion of a son of Mr. Woolley. That son is now a Methodist minister in Canada, from which country he sends Mr. Cook the cheering tidings. A Hull firm write to say that they are large employers of labour, and that some years previously a young man left their service in the ordinary way, and they heard and thought nothing of him afterwards. But the writers said that he had just waited upon them with ten shillings, which he stated was the value of some things of theirs which he purloined from them when in their service; and he alleged that he did this because he had been converted at Mr. Cook's mission in that town. The ten shillings were enclosed as a gift from the firm to the fund which maintains the Evangelist.

Here is good news from Barrow-in-Furness. The Rev. W May writes: "The good work is still going on. You will remember that several railway men got converted during the mission, and they are giving evidence of the genuineness of their conversion. Through their influence a revival has commenced among the men employed on the line between here and Whitehaven, and eighteen have decided for Christ." This shows how the good work extends, and how one conversion, like a wave of the sea, begets another. Three months later, additional evidence of this arrives. A minister writes: "You will remember Captain ———, who was converted at your men's meeting. He has just returned from a dangerous voyage. When his ship was in imminent peril, but whilst the storm was raging, he astonished the crew by declaring that if death came to him it was all right, as he had faith in God. Twenty-two of the crew were converted to God during the voyage." And here is still more good news from the sea, which will be as invigorating to the soul as a good sea-breeze is to the body The same correspondent says: "We continue to receive cheering news of The Captain's success as a preacher of the gospel amongst the sailors. A few weeks since we heard that at Port Said he had led thirty of the sailors to Christ."

A young Cornishman writes from a large city house in London to say that four years ago he was brought to God during the mission services Mr. Cook held in Truro. It was the turning-point in his life, and he expresses the greatest thankfulness that he was made a partaker of that grace which alone " can foil the tempter's power," before he migrated from a quiet Cornish town to the metropolis. A sister writes from Birmingham to say that her brother has recently died in the faith, and that his conversion was due to the mission Mr. Cook held in that town. Thus was another sheaf gathered in. A gentleman writes from the west of England to express his indebtedness to Mr. Cook, and he encloses five pounds as 'a present, begging the Evangelist to accept it.' This, however, Mr. Cook was unable to do, as it would have violated one of his rules, which is to receive no gifts of money lest the ministry be blamed. A Cambridge man informs the Evangelist that for months past he had been praying for purifying grace, and by accident was led to enter Hobson Street Chapel, Cambridge, on a Sunday afternoon when Mr. Cook was holding a men's service. He states that he felt the power of the Holy Spirit so much in the service that he shook from head to foot, every nerve was at work, and he was obliged to yield to the influence of the gracious Spirit. The Rev. R. Crawford Johnson writes from Dublin to say that a member of the choir, who was saved at the Dublin mission, had recently died, and died a triumphant death. His last regret was that he had not won a single soul for Christ, and he besought his wife with his dying breath to give him the joy of winning her, and thus he passed away beyond the reach of temptation. A gentleman writes from the same city, and says that a friend of his, a member of the Irish Church, dined with him at his house on Sunday, and told him that he and one of his "chums" had been saved at this Dublin mission. The possibility of a conscious salvation was to this good man something incredible, and now that he had obtained it the strangeness of his new experience made his conversation most interesting.

We shall have to speak of the labours of our Evangelist amongst the young immediately, but we may add here that the proprietress of a ladies' school in Ireland sends word of a great "tide of blessing" which had swept over her establishment as the result of one of Mr. Cook's missions. Eight members of her household, who were trusting Christ before, had received a fuller baptism of the Holy Spirit; two backsliders had been recovered; two servants were saved; two others were seeking salvation, and the lady's own soul had been filled with God. She adds: "The home is to-day a heaven upon earth. A nephew has also come to Jesus, and three other friends have received an increase of blessing. To God be all the glory." An Exeter correspondent sends intelligence of the death of one of the converts of the Exeter mission who "sweetly fell asleep in Jesus," and whose conversion was followed by the conversion of her husband on the second Sunday after the close of the mission, which event led to the conversion of a daughter; and thus wife, husband, and child were "bound together in the bundle of life." Tidings come from Exmouth to the effect that a young lady went into Exeter at the invitation of a lady to attend Mr. Cook's mission, and was brought to God. She in her turn prayed for the conversion of two friends, one of whom found salvation at a subsequent service, while the other obtained the blessing in her own room. Thus does "Jesus ride on," and in this way will He continue to "ride on" till "all are subdued."

References have been made to the Dublin mission, and now it should be stated that God graciously owned Mr. Cook's work among the pupils of Wesley College in that city. Here are a dozen letters from boys who, at the time of writing, were resident pupils of the College, and who all testify to the saving power of Christ which they experienced at the mission. Thomas Cook himself was, as we have seen, converted to God when a boy, and this circumstance has encouraged him to look for like instances of saving grace among his youthful hearers. Nor has he looked in vain.

Is there a spot in the world from which tidings of this kind would be more welcome to ministerial readers than from Kingswood School, Bath, where the sons of Wesleyan ministers are educated. The writer had a brief experience of Woodhouse Grove School, and is well aware of the temptations to which such life exposes boys when they are at an impressionable age, and when they are more afraid of being thought good, and of professing to be good, than of anything else that could possibly happen to them. There is reason to believe that girls have to endure the same temptations in their schools, however well conducted the schools may be; and hence it is impossible for praying parents, who send their children from home to be educated, not to have some misgiving about the wisdom of that particular course. The late Mrs. Booth strongly deprecated the boarding-school system, as all readers of her books must know, and certainly the results of her own conduct in training her children herself have justified much of what she wrote.

The sons of Methodist preachers are not without their advantages, neither are they without their disadvantages. Their fathers are usually out when the sons' school hours are over, their homes are constantly broken up, and it is often necessary for them to be left behind when their parents are compelled to change their Circuits. There is a popular impression that the sons of ministers "fall" more frequently than the sons of others. This is a delusion, partly accounted for by the fact that every such "fall" naturally excites attention, like a falling star, while the cases of those who stand give rise to no comment. The writer not long since took part in a Home Missionary meeting in South Wales, when three of the chief speakers happened to be Wesleyan ministers' sons and Woodhouse Grove boys. Yet the circumstance was only regarded as natural and unimportant. But if three sons of ministers had appeared together on the stage of the theatre in that town, all the world would have heard of it! Grace, however, is not hereditary, and hence preachers do well to be solicitous lest their ministry should be discredited by their own children. Those who were present at a recent Conference, when our beloved brother Champness prayed for "our own children," will not have forgotten the intense fervour and many tears with which the brethren responded when he said, "They are not all *good*, Lord, but they are *ours;* save them, we beseech Thee!" These observations will prepare the way for the extracts we now give from two letters written by the Rev. Dr. Bowden, governor of Kingswood School, referring to the results of visits paid by our Evangelist to the school. In May 1887, Dr. Bowden writes: "On Tuesday evening I had the library full, and took down fifty-five names of those who did not previously meet in class. Mr. Richards held a meeting for junior inquirers on Wednesday, and I had a meeting for seniors on Thursday. The library was crowded. I am encouraging them to help each other. The demand by separate groups for places for prayer almost passes our accommodation. Groups of boys from twelve to fourteen, and seniors with juniors gathered round them, meet for prayer. On Friday two boys in the middle of the school came and acknowledged misconduct, and made restitution. That was a blessed feast of repentance. Many thanks for your blessed visit. The whole tone of our life is raised. It was good, but is now much better." In September 1890, Dr. Bowden writes: "The library quite full with my class, and the new candidates for membership. I took down twenty-eight new names for Mr. Richard's class and my own. The old members are quickened, and the boys whose names I took are among some whose only hope is converting grace."

At Trinity Hall Mr. Cook has been permitted to reap sheaves also. Many of the girls in that establishment were savingly converted on the occasion of a visit he paid them some few years ago, and the tradition still lingers in the school of the wonderful gale of grace that swept over the pupils at that time. These circumstances will cause the hearts of all Methodist preachers to turn towards the Evangelist with peculiar tenderness and affection, for it often happens that ministers' children receive less attention than the children of others, because it is supposed that they need less; whereas they require, if not more, certainly quite as much. "That our sons may be as plants grown up in their youth; that our daughters may be as corner-stones, polished after the similitude of a palace."

Amongst pupils in private schools also God has given Mr. Cook many souls for his hire. The proprietors of such schools have often a groundless fear of the parents of their pupils being offended if efforts are made by evangelists to secure the conversion of the pupils; and, no doubt, some discretion is needed in work of this kind. No more shall be said here, therefore, except that there lie before the writer three beautiful letters written by girls in the same private school, all telling of conversion, and of the conversions of sisters and school-fellows, the results of one of Mr. Cook's missions.

The daughter of one of our ablest deceased ministers sends encouraging news of the perseverance in the Christian life of a number of girls who were brought to God at a mission which Mr. Cook held twelve months before the letter was written. The anniversary of their conversion was observed in the Society-class, and the lady leader assures the Evangelist that they are standing fast in the Lord. This batch of young converts was divided into two Society-classes, and the lady who writes was made leader of both, and thus the girls had the great advantage of intelligent and loving instruction given week by week in the deeper things of God.

Something has been said (in the chapter on holiness-meetings) of the prominence which Mr. Cook everywhere gives to holiness, and much might be written concerning the great blessing which numbers of Christian people have found through the teaching given by our Evangelist on these occasions. Many Christians are full of thankfulness because they have been led by Mr. Cook into that rest " where pure enjoyment reigns," and " God is loved alone." Their testimonies are of great value. Mr. Wesley attached much importance to such experiences, and published as many of them as he could in his immortal *Journals;* and the writer believes that if full particulars were given of the way in which some modern Methodists and others have been made witnesses of God's power to save unto the uttermost, good would be done. Correspondents speak of a lean Christian experience possessed before they obtained the fuller life of entire sanctification. They confess the weary struggles, the disappointments, the failures of their previous Christian life, and they praise God for lifting them into a higher and clearer atmosphere, where " His commandments " are not felt to be " grievous."

Professor Drummond has said nothing wiser than this : " The difficulties of the Christian life arise from this — we attempt to half-live it." When that life is *wholly* lived, it is easy, delightful, and grateful, as much of the correspondence shows which has grown out of the series of holiness-meetings which Mr. Cook has held in many parts of the United Kingdom during the last ten years.

All Mr. Cook's "seals of apostleship" are not in the British Isles, nor are all the subjects of Her Majesty. He has some converts in Norway, in which country, in company with Dr. Wood, he held a mission in the year 1886. During the Cardiff mission, Mr. Cook met with a Norwegian minister belonging to the Methodist Episcopal Church of America, who besought him to go to Norway and preach the gospel to his countrymen. The introduction of Methodism into Norway is an interesting story, having the ring of Wesley's *Journals* about it. Briefly, it is this. A Norwegian sailor named Petersen settled in America, and was converted through attending a Methodist class-meeting, as I have known Norwegians, and Danes, and Germans, and Dutchmen to be converted in Hull through attending Methodist services. Petersen's conversion was a thorough one, and when, therefore, soon afterwards, he paid a visit to his native land, he did precisely what a hundred years previously John Nelson did at Birstall, and with like results. His testimony produced a deep impression, many of his neighbours sought salvation, and the neighbourhood became aroused. Then Petersen was obliged to return to America, but the fire he had kindled did not go out. On the contrary, it spread, and that with such rapidity that the services of a minister for the little flock became a necessity, and urgent requests were sent to the American Conference for one to be appointed. Eventually Petersen himself was ordained, and sent as the first minister of the Church which he had founded. That was in the year 1850, since which time the mission has made such progress that now it reports three thousand five hundred members, over three thousand Sunday-school scholars, and thirty-three ministers.

Mr. Cook and Dr. Wood went to Tönsberg, which is one of the oldest towns in Norway, and where there is a Methodist chapel, which will hold, perhaps, two hundred and fifty people. They entered upon their work with fear and trembling, being quite ignorant of the language. Dr. Wood, having spoken in Paris through an interpreter, was the first speaker at this Norwegian service, the native minister acting as interpreter. Dr. Wood had not spoken long before it was made evident that a great blessing was coming. The interpreter, Pastor Jorgensen, was in full sympathy with the evangelists, and hence gave the spirit of their addresses as well as the letter.

At first the good Norwegians did not understand what Mr. Cook wished them to do when he invited them to come to the communion rail to seek salvation. But in course of time they caught his idea, and then fell in with it as readily as do English people. The power of God rested upon the congregation, and ignorance of the language did not prevent the evangelists from doing much good work for God. One afternoon, when those who were seeking Christ were asked to stand up, nearly half the congregation responded, and in the evening of the same day twenty-five persons knelt at the rail seeking pardon in old-fashioned Methodist style. The interpreter knelt between the Evangelist and the penitents, and by his mouth the Evangelist dealt with them and led them to Christ.

Very touching it was to see the people praying with tearful faces and in a language unknown to the evangelists, and then to watch the change that transfigured them when they realised the forgiving love of God. In many ways the simple-minded Norwegians tried to express their gratitude to the evangelists. They would point upwards and then point to themselves, in order to intimate that they had been brought into communion with heaven. One woman, who knew a little broken English, said, "*You* make my heart weary; *He* (pointing to the sky) make my heart peace." After a few days the evangelists were obliged to tear themselves away from these loving people. They left at five o'clock A.M., but though the hour was so early, about twenty of the natives were present to say good-bye, and to urge the evangelists to come again, which they promised to do, in case the cloud should lead that way.

This mission in Norway was held more than five years ago, but during this year a Bradford Methodist, well known to the writer, travelling in Norway, met the native minister in his own land who interpreted for Mr. Cook and Dr. Wood, and heard from his lips of the good work that has been done, and is still being done, in that favourite land of tourists, by " the people called Methodists." Mr. Cook thinks that the fields are white unto the harvest in Norway, and that what is needed is, that reapers should go thither, and put in the sickle, where good "wages" may be obtained, and much "fruit unto eternal life" may be gathered. And it is perhaps worth while to note that Mr. Cook's experience in Norway has confirmed a theory which he has long held, that it is possible to preach the gospel with saving power through an interpreter. If life be spared, Mr. Cook will test this theory again in other parts of the world, if the Lord will.

What " popular " minister is there who would not willingly throw the most splendid popularity to the winds, if in exchange for it he could taste the joy of leading sinners to Christ ? Purses of gold, illuminated addresses, silver tea-services, timepieces, and gold watches are not to be despised when they are presented to pastors by kind and grateful friends when the pastoral tie is about to be broken. But who of us is there, no matter how heavily laden he may be with such testimonials, who would not sacrifice all he has received for " letters of commendation " such as St. Paul wrote about, and such as this chapter deals with ? If our ministry is barren, what *can* compensate us for our service ? Not money; for other callings are far more lucrative. Not applause ; for what will it profit us, though our praises are sounded in the newspapers every week, and our services are greatly in request ? When the ear is filled with dust,—as soon it must be,—of what avail will it be that many admiring people chaffer about our eloquence, and learning, and oratorical gifts ? But it is written : " They that be wise shall shine as the brightness of the firmament ; and they that turn many to righteousness, as the stars for ever and ever."

The reader will not complain if I close this chapter with another quotation from Dr. Dale. He is addressing preachers, and his theme is " Evangelistic Power."

" Those of us who have reason to believe that God has called us to walk in obscurer paths (than those in which eminent evangelists walk), and to render Him a less brilliant service, may with reverence and humility ask for a larger measure of this special form of grace than most of us have received. God will not rebuke us for presumption, if, in the presence of vast masses of human ignorance and misery, and vice and irreligion, on which we are able to make hardly any impression, we entreat Him to grant us some of the force which He has granted in such a wonderful measure to illustrious evangelists. Or if for any reason this cannot be, we may still implore Him to bestow it on some of our brethren. Whether the work is done by ourselves or by others, it matters not: but we ought to pray incessantly that the work may be done."

CHAPTER X.

CORNISH REVIVALS.

CORNWALL is, as all the world knows, *the* Methodist county. As one of the most distinguished and best informed of Cornish Methodists said to the writer when driving to a Home Missionary meeting in the Porthleven Circuit, "Methodism has done everything for Cornwall."

If there is one spot in God's universe on which, more than on any other, it might be written with propriety, "Methodism—her mark," that spot is Cornwall.

Notwithstanding all the efforts that have been made by the creation of the See of Truro to convert our people from "schism," there are still upwards of twenty thousand members (including probationers) of Society in that county, besides an innumerable number of adherents; and this despite the unprecedented migrations of recent years. There is reason to believe that not for many years—perhaps never, all things considered—has Methodism been in a healthier and more prosperous condition in Cornwall than it is at the present time. The prospect, therefore, of the extinction of Methodism in that western county is as remote as it was prior to the erection of Truro Cathedral.

It is well known that Cornwall is remarkable for its extraordinary revivals, which revivals take place not only in Methodist chapels, but in churches, where "parsons," as well as others, get converted, and are carried on the shoulders of rejoicing "workers," fittingly so called. No doubt some of the stories that are in circulation about Cornish revivals would be nailed to the counter if strict justice were meted out, and the writer would indeed blush for shame if he were to add to the number of such tales. He will, however, endeavour to keep his pen well in hand, and to write "as the oracles of God, that God in all things may be glorified through Jesus Christ."

Ordinarily the Methodist services in Cornwall are as decorous and quiet as they are in London, but *occasionally* the most wonderful things occur in that county, when, as the phrase is, "a revival breaks out." It is still no uncommon thing for a large chapel in Cornwall to be kept open every night for a month, or even six weeks, and to be crowded with worshippers, without the attraction of any strange preacher, and notwithstanding the paucity of the population, when the Spirit of God is poured out and sinners are being converted. For example, Mr Cook held a mission in St. Austell last year, and the Superintendent of the Circuit, writing a few months afterwards, says: "Not less than a thousand persons amongst the various sections of Methodism have been converted *since the mission closed, and the work still goes on.*" When it is remembered that the entire population of St. Austell and the adjacent villages is a mere drop in a bucket in comparison, say, with the population of Hackney, or Islington, or Bethnal Green, it will be seen that this is an instance of a sweeping revival. Were a revival to "break out" in London that should affect a similar proportion of our five millions of people, the record of the Book of the Acts of the Apostles would be completely broken, and new light would be thrown on that expression which speaks of "a nation" being "born in a day." Oh, that the things which God has done in Cornwall may be done in our own city! Then would the ears of the Lord's enemies tingle, while His own people would be like them that dream. Then would our mouth be "filled with laughter, and our tongue with singing;" then would they say "among the heathen, The Lord hath done great things for them."

The thoughtful reader will do well to be on his guard lest incredulous friends persuade him to believe that these Cornish revivals are evanescent in their effects. Some of them are as ephemeral as the revival of Pentecost, and as the Evangelical Revival of the eighteenth century.

Alarmists tell us that the English coal-fields are being gradually exhausted, which is likely enough, seeing that the great Atlantic liners force nearly three hundred tons of coal through their boiler-fires every day. What is worse, they tell us that the sun himself is being gradually cooled, and that the time will come when the sun will be as cold as ice. I was naturally uneasy lest this catastrophe should happen in my time, until I chanced to read that it was calculated that the sun's heat would last about eighteen million more years, and then I took heart of grace, thinking that the danger was not urgent.

"God's in His heaven,
All's right with the world."

There need be no hesitation in saying that when the coal-fields are used up, and the sun has ceased to shine, the effects of some of these extraordinary revivals in Cornwall will be as fresh as the dew of the morning.

It was the privilege of the writer, some years ago, to be the guest of Mr. W Bickford-Smith, M.P., at Trevarno. Seated with him in his library, the conversation turned on the subject of Cornish revivals and their accompanying phenomena, and I ventured to ask Mr. Bickford-Smith how far these extraordinary movements had, in his opinion, promoted the permanent extension of the work of God in Cornwall. He told me that in his judgment their effect upon the work of God had been far-reaching and lasting, and in proof of this statement he added that his father, the late Dr. Smith, the Methodist historian, was himself converted during a revival in the Wesleyan Chapel at Camborne, on which occasion the place was kept open every night for six successive weeks.

Writing in 1767, Mr. Wesley says in the preface to the third volume of his *Journals*: "I am sensible there are many particulars in the ensuing Journal which some serious persons will not believe, and which others will turn to ridicule. But this I cannot help, unless by concealing those things which I believe it my bounden duty to declare I cannot do otherwise while I am persuaded that this was a real work of God, and that He hath so wrought this and all His marvellous works that they ought to be had in remembrance."

The circumstances related in the following pages are, no doubt, strange, but they describe "a real work of God," and they are published for the same reasons as were Wesley's *Journals*.

Mr. Cook had his first experience of the Cornish character before he became a Connexional Evangelist, when he was holding a mission with the Rev. E. Davidson at New Marske. During the course of that mission a man came out to seek salvation, which he did with intense earnestness. He literally "howled" for mercy, if the use of that word may be forgiven, which perhaps it may, seeing that it is found in the Authorised Version, and continued to do so for the space of half-an-hour. He then rolled over on his back, and kicked as well as shouted, until at length he was quite exhausted. After a while he raised himself gradually, meantime exclaiming, in a mournful tone, "It's coming, it's coming," and attempting, as it were, to grasp with both hands something which none but himself saw. Presently he appeared to secure what he was seeking, and, jumping to his feet, he began to praise God with a loud voice and to dance for joy. He then rushed down the aisle, and, by clearing several pews, reached his wife, whom he affectionately embraced in the presence of the congregation, and said, "Praise the Lord, I am saved." He then turned his attention to Mr. Cook, and appeared to be about to treat him in the same manner, but by a strategic movement the Evangelist eluded his embrace, and then bided his time till he could congratulate the convert with safety on his remarkable conversion, which must have been on a par with those "powerful" conversions of which our fellow-Methodists in the United States speak. This and other episodes with which Mr. Cook met during his early days, led him to expect that when he visited Cornwall he should see strange things. His first mission in Cornwall was a disappointment to him, and presumably to the people also, and the writer heard it stated at the time that "Thomas Cook could do nothing in Cornwall." This first mission was held in the spacious chapel at Penzance, and it may as well be plainly said, that the good people of Penzance were not prepared for so young a preacher,—they desired an ex-President,—and did not approve of his innovations. The writer has been privileged to address Methodist congregations from Peterhead to Penzance, and he may perhaps be permitted to say, without being charged with any impropriety, that nowhere has he found a congregation which has impressed him more with its intelligence and piety and numbers, than has the magnificent congregation which worships in the Penzance Wesleyan Chapel. It is not surprising that these excellent people did not easily recover from the shock they received when first they saw the youthful mission preacher, and that they complained that "the Conference had sent them a lad." The singing-band, and especially the lantern which Mr. Cook used in the streets, were a rock of offence, and the comment made by the good Cornish folk was, "We don't belong to do that way here." The roughs, emulating the "wild beasts" of Ephesus and of Eastbourne, but coming far short of the latter in their violence, threw stones at the lantern, and for a while the Evangelist and his methods were unpopular, not only outside the chapel, but inside also. The "workers" almost struck, they certainly ceased to work; and when the Evangelist urged them to get him a larger congregation, they said in reply, "Get some folks saved, and then others will come of their own accord," which, as it happens to be a doctrine of our own, we will not contradict. God, however, was with "the lad," and, despite the aloofness of the people, at least a hundred inquirers' names were taken. Had the church worked cordially with "the lad," the one hundred converts might have been a thousand! This they would not do, and the result was that, although the mission cannot be called a failure, it was one of the most disappointing missions Mr. Cook has ever conducted, especially if regard be had to the high expectations he had cherished concerning the possibilities of work in Cornwall.

We intimated in an earlier chapter that it was owing to their want of the attribute of omniscience that the "July Committee" declined to recommend Mr. Cook when he first offered himself to the Wesleyan Conference as a candidate for the ministry. Doubtless it was owing to a similar defect that the good people of Penzance held aloof from "the lad" when he first went to reap in Cornwall. Critics who can see the end from the beginning will, of course, blame the unwisdom both of the Committee and of the Cornish congregation.

After an interval of two years, Mr. Cook paid a second visit to Cornwall, the seat of war this time being Truro. Church influence was at that time powerful in Truro, as well it might be, considering that among a small population of, perhaps, fourteen thousand souls, the Church of England had twenty "priests" at work. The Cathedral was also in course of erection, and as the material building threatened to overshadow St. Mary's Chapel, which is hard by, so timid hearts feared lest Church of Englandism proper should absorb Church of Englandism *felt*, as Methodism has not unfittingly been called.

The situation was made the more grave, by the fact that Methodism in Truro had suffered some years' leanness, and that two or three Methodist families had, for reasons best known to themselves, forsaken the Church of their fathers.

Dr. Wood, of Southport, accompanied Mr. Cook, and acted as his fellow-labourer throughout the mission, especially helping in the inquiry-room.

The first Sunday-morning service was a time of great blessing. The Evangelist's theme was entire sanctification, and the congregation were visibly and deeply affected by the Word. Hardly had the preacher finished his sermon when a well-known local preacher rose and asked leave to say a few words. Permission being given, he said in substance as follows: " I stand up before the congregation to testify that while you have been preaching, sir, I have been enabled to say, ' I claim the blessing *now*,' with the result that ' the blood of Jesus Christ, His Son, cleanseth *me* from all sin.'" The effect of this most unusual occurrence on a Cornish congregation may be imagined. A glorious work instantly began. The interest spread until the spacious edifice was crowded night after night. The Parliamentary election was proceeding at the time, and it may be stated as a proof of the hold which the mission took of the people, that on the evening when the poll was declared, the candidate being Mr. W Bickford-Smith, a distinguished member of their own clan, the chapel was crowded, and remained crowded, the people truly enough supposing that religion is of more importance than politics.

Some wonderful scenes were witnessed at this Truro mission. Conviction of sin was made a reality, and the conversions appeared to be thorough. However strange it may seem to cold-blooded persons who have never shed a tear over their sins, it is true to say that many of the converts when seeking forgiveness from God writhed and struggled as in great bodily distress, and became so exhausted that they had to be supported on their way home. In addition to the usual meetings for men and women and young people, a special service was held on each market-day for the country people. On the second market-day of the mission five hundred persons were present in the afternoon at a busy hour, and the power of God was present to heal. The Rev. R. Allen writes: "On the last night of the mission the new converts were invited to tea, and arrangements were made for placing them in Society-classes. The meeting was held in the chapel, the converts occupying the centre. Seldom has a grander sight been witnessed than was seen when the converts rose together to confess their faith in Christ. More than three hundred and fifty persons above fourteen years of age were enrolled as inquirers, and seventy-five under that age. Amongst the converts there are persons from all the Churches in the city and many from the adjacent district. Such a work of God has not been seen in this city for many years."

The reader will be interested to know that a stained-glass window was placed in the Truro Wesleyan Chapel by the converts to commemorate the great blessing received by them during the mission, and there it remains to this day as a memorial unto the Lord.

Mr. Cook next visited Camborne, and here also the

arm of the Lord was revealed. On the Saturday previous to the mission he met "the workers," four hundred being present, and gave them definite instructions about the conduct of the campaign.

Warned by his experience two years earlier at Penzance, the Evangelist was careful to insist upon implicit obedience to his directions, promising the people that if they would obey his orders he would take the responsibility of the mission. Happily there was a leader of men present, ready to show the rest how to follow. This was Captain Josiah Thomas, whose praise is in all the Cornish Churches. He unhesitatingly declared that he would do as he was told, and, as men are gregarious in their habits, the other "workers" intimated their readiness to follow his example, and thus there was a prospect that the mission would get under weigh with a favourable breeze. "Is he one of we?" asked the good Camborne people about their mission preacher, for it is well known that of all her Majesty's subjects the Cornish folks love themselves the best. Thomas Cook was not "one of we;" but tidings had reached Camborne of the success that God had graciously vouchsafed to His servant at Truro, and the Camborne friends were not unwilling to believe that what the Evangelist had been enabled to do in their cathedral city he would be permitted to do also in their own town.

At the close of the first Sunday-evening service Mr. Cook asked the leaders and local preachers and other workers to retire to the inquiry-rooms, whither he would direct the penitents to follow them. This, however, was a great trial to their faith. They were looking for an old-fashioned Methodist prayer-meeting, and when they were directed to leave the chapel in quietness, and that before a single person had intimated his intention of coming out as a penitent, it seemed to them they were being asked to step upon nothing, and in astonishment they asked, "What is he going to do? How will he manage the prayer-meeting without us?" Captain Josiah Thomas, however, led the way and the others followed, murmuring to themselves as they went in their own dialect, "We don't belong to do this way here."

> "Forward, the Light Brigade!
> Was there a man dismayed?
> Not tho' the soldier knew
> Some one had *blundered*
> Theirs not to make reply,
> Theirs not to reason why,
> Theirs but to do and die."

Into the inquiry room walked the one hundred. When they found themselves in the inquiry-room, and not a single convert with them, and knew that the service was proceeding quietly in the chapel, they smiled at the folly of the young preacher, who had dared to introduce such innovations into a place where revival services were as well understood as the multiplication table. But God did not fail His servant. About half-a-dozen persons found peace with God that night, and the success of the mission was insured. The next evening the number of converts was larger; the following evening it was larger still, and so the work continued to spread, and the workers became reconciled to new methods, and said, "God is with the preacher; we will work with him."

They kept their word. Never has the Evangelist laboured with a more loyal and devoted people. Soon the spacious chapel became too small for the congregation even on the week-evenings. Often was it crowded an hour before the time when the service was announced to begin, and a messenger was sent to the preacher's home asking him to go at once and begin the service, as it was useless to keep the crowd waiting in the chapel. The Rev. W. Haslam truly says: "Cornish revivals are things by themselves." Mr. Cook's experience confirms this statement. It is impossible adequately to describe what took place in this wonderful Camborne mission. If an attempt were made to do this, and if it were only partially successful, probably few readers would give full credence to the account; and therefore I will stay my hand, and be content to indicate merely one or two features of the work. In the midst of the sermon a shriek would suddenly be heard, and when the innocent preacher asked what it meant, the person who had made it would answer, "My Tom has been tak'n down," or "My Jim," as the case might be. The voice would often be that of a mother or wife, and the explanation of it was that the son or husband had been convinced of sin, and had given some outward sign of his distress. Mr. Cook would then direct the stricken one to be led to the inquiry-room, which would be no sooner done than another would be seized in the same way, and another shriek would rend the heavens, and then another, and another, until it became impossible to proceed with the sermon. Sometimes a person would cry out audibly, "Lord, save me." One evening a man made a thrill run through the chapel as he uttered this exclamation, meantime running down the aisle as though he were actually escaping for his life. He was followed by a second, and then by a third, and so on till perhaps fifty persons ran the gauntlet of the crowded congregation, and found refuge in the inquiry-rooms. There the scenes were simply awful in their impressiveness, although occasionally the element of ludicrousness was not absent.

Not to cry was impossible, so acute was the distress of the penitents. It was equally impossible not to laugh at times, so ludicrous did the situation appear. Strong men wept and perspired, as well they might do, seeing that they threw their bodies into all kinds of contortions, and literally rolled on the floor, and, in no metaphorical sense, writhed in pain. In the women's room it was much the same. The cries of the women were so piercing that few can imagine what they were like who have not been accustomed to such vehement demonstrations. Then, when they had found salvation, the women would praise God as loudly as they could, and dance round the room, hugging their sisters, and calling upon them for help to praise God for His mercy. Never before did the Evangelist understand the force of the personal pronoun when applied to this solemn matter. "*I* am His," one would say; "Jesus died for *me*," another would exclaim; and thus new light was cast upon many of the verses in our incomparable hymn-book. It is worthy of remark that Cornish penitents will not be satisfied with any human assurance of pardon; nothing comforts them but the witness of God's Holy Spirit. "When I am saved, I shall *know* it," was almost the invariable cry of the penitent; nor was it possible to show that this was an unscriptural requirement.

Some would wrestle for hours for this assurance and if they did not get it, they would leave the chapel and come again the following evening and "renew the glorious strife." Not seldom the service would last from six o'clock to eleven o'clock, although, as most people know, Mr. Cook's services are usually much briefer than such services commonly are. Even at eleven o'clock it was difficult to induce the people to leave the sacred place. "We want to be saved," they would say, when directed to leave, owing to the lateness of the hour, and it was only by turning off the gas that it was possible to dismiss the remnant. At one of the services Mr. Cook selected as his text the words, "And whosoever will, let him take the water of life freely." When he asked, "Who will take the water of life to-night?" a voice answered, "I will," and soon scores of voices were heard all over the chapel saying, "I will, I will." Blessed be God for such instances of holy enthusiasm! Our places of worship often seem to be ice-houses. If we want fire, we must go to the Exchange or to the political meeting. But when the Spirit of the Lord is copiously poured out, coldness and conventionalities are destroyed, and the sacred fire begins to burn. The Spirit of judgment is also the Spirit of burning, and when He is allowed free scope, He will kindle enthusiasm. Professor Huxley may sneer at what he learnedly calls "corybantic religion," but his sneers will not affect us. May God in His mercy save the Churches from a religion that would be according to the mind of Professor Huxley! *Fire* is what the Churches need. May God baptize us all with it, and then we shall burn our way into the hearts of sinners!

At one of the evening services of this Camborne mission the sermon was not needed, so deep was the earnestness of the people, and the names of fifty inquirers were taken without any discourse being delivered. Often would a son or daughter find the treasure in the inquiry-room, and then return to the chapel for father or mother and lead the loved one to the newly-found Saviour. A deep impression was made one evening by a young man who returned to the chapel from the inquiry-room, and, with uplifted hands, said in a loud whisper, "He is mine, He is mine," repeating the words many times as though in a rapture of joy. In cold type the incident may seem unimpressive, but if the reader remembers that it took place in the midst of a congregation of fifteen hundred Cornish people, all of whom were in a state of holy religious excitement, he will understand how it is that the spectators think that they never shall forget the scene and the impression it made upon them at the time. Many people came to the Camborne Chapel during that mission who had walked some miles in order to be present, and who came with the one object of seeking salvation. "Put us into a front pew," they would say to the pew-opener, for they desired to make their passage to the inquiry-room as easy as might be.

The afternoon meetings were seasons of great blessing. Occasionally there would be heard what the initiated call "the holy laugh," and this at first somewhat shocked the Evangelist. We have all read in our Bibles of the mouths of God's people being "filled with laughter," but we have such a horror of "corybantic religion" that we are scandalised at any extraordinary outbursts of religious joy. However, Captain Josiah Thomas, who had done something at first to reconcile the people to the Evangelist's methods, now reconciled the Evangelist to the people's peculiarities. He assured Mr. Cook that however loud and sudden the laugh might be, it was not irreverent, but was simply the expression of overwhelming joy in the Holy Ghost. God gave His servant great power over the people. The quiet way in which he spoke, and the effects that followed, filled the people with awe, and compelled them to exclaim, "We never saw it on this fashion."

At the quarterly meeting held soon after the close of the mission, the superintendent minister reported that during the few preceding weeks, over one thousand persons had publicly decided for Christ in Camborne. As we have seen, many of the converts came from the vicinity; nevertheless it must be admitted that for a thousand conversions to take place in three or four weeks in a town where the entire population would not probably exceed eight or ten thousand souls, was an extraordinary occurrence, and one likely to make that period henceforth a month to be "much observed unto the Lord."

Here is a strange incident. Twenty-eight years before the Camborne mission, a little girl lost half a sovereign, and was convinced that a certain man who was in her company at the time had picked it up. When, however, the man was taxed with the theft, he denied it, and, as it could not be proved against him, the matter dropped. The little girl became the wife of a Cornish tradesman, and the suspected man continued to live. When the mission was held the man attended and was converted, and it was the pleasure of the Rev. E. O. Coleman to receive the confession of this changed man, and to take the half-sovereign to the lady in his name; thus restitution was made. A circumstance like this shows that time does not affect sin when once it is committed. What matters it whether the sin was committed yesterday or eight-and-twenty years ago? Let the reader observe how this occurrence confirms the teaching of the late Bishop Magee in his valuable treatise on "The Atonement." That learned prelate writes: "The remarkable fact connected with the punishment inflicted by the conscience is, that it seems to have in it nothing of the nature of expiation or satisfaction. No amount of pain of this kind that we suffer seems to satisfy it. It inflicts and re-inflicts, and inflicts again, the same torment every time the cruel memory drags us within its range. The man who has sinned against himself, against the inner law of his truer and better nature, cannot feel that in all the agonies of his self-reproach there is any expiation. This prison of an offended conscience is one out of which there is no escape, because no one farthing of the debt of remorse can ever be fully paid."

In our libraries we read; in the inquiry-room we test and confirm what we read; as the medical student proves his theories by "walking the hospitals."

In Helston, also, Mr. Cook held a mission which God abundantly blessed. The fine new chapel was opened a short time before the mission began, not without some misgivings on the part of good friends, who feared that the dimensions of the structure were larger than the needs of the town demanded. But the "house-warming" which took place when the mission was held in the chapel gave the new building a capital start. Many of the Camborne scenes were repeated, and numbers of interesting conversions occurred. Amongst the converts was a man who, when he entered the inquiry-room, cast himself down upon the floor, and cried mightily to God for pardon, moving on his knees up and down the room while so doing. For three hours he continued to do this, and then he retired, not having obtained the blessing. The following evening he came again, and, taking off his coat, he placed it on the floor and used it as a mat, having on the previous evening hurt his knees by his exertions. But the coat was soon left in the rear, as the poor fellow in his excitement moved about from one part of the room to another, seeking rest and finding none. He asked for a glass of water, which was given him, to quench his thirst; then he asked for another, and drank it in an instant. So protracted did the struggle become, and so exhausting, that the Circuit minister kindly brought the penitent man a cup of cocoa, and this also he quickly swallowed. At length deliverance came, and the people of God joined the convert in praising the Lord who had made the bones which He had broken to rejoice. We have read in our New Testaments of one who "laboured fervently in prayer." Here is an illustration of the apostle's meaning. At Liskeard, also, God gave Mr. Cook some sheaves. The work here was not so demonstrative as at Camborne, but it appeared to be deep and thorough. On the evening of the last night of the Liskeard mission, the Evangelist waited long for four elderly men to surrender themselves to God, but they hesitated to do so. For their sakes he protracted the service till a late hour, for it seemed to him that if they hardened their hearts that night, they might never enter into God's rest. The objects of his solicitude would neither leave the chapel nor leave their pews, and so prayer was offered for their salvation. Eventually one of the number took the decisive step, then another followed suit, the remaining two maintaining an attitude of resistance. But the service did not close until all four had given proof of their determination to serve the Lord. "And of some have compassion, making a difference; and others save with fear, pulling them out of the fire."

St. Austell was also visited by Mr. Cook, the time being spent there chiefly in seeking to effect the reconversion of the Church. The meetings for Christians were much blessed, and did much to prepare the way for the work that followed the mission. Not more than eighty persons publicly avowed themselves as new disciples of the Lord Jesus, but a fire was kindled which set, not only the town, but the Circuit also in a blaze. Several times whilst the Evangelist was preaching the Word at St. Austell, persons called out audibly for mercy; and although this may seem a small thing, it is conceivable that if such things occurred in certain places of worship, known to the reader as well as to the writer, the congregations would be almost as much astonished as they would if the stones were to cry out. At one of the services an inquirer went into the vestry to seek salvation, and returned to the chapel rejoicing in God before the service was over. He proceeded audibly to praise God for His saving grace, and then exhorted the unconverted to do as he had done, calling upon some by name, and giving point to his entreaties by bewailing his folly in wasting forty years in the service of Satan. It will readily be believed that incidents like these prevented the services from being dull, and helped to keep the congregations wide-awake.

The following extracts from letters written by the superintendent minister, the Rev T. D. Anderson, B.A., will serve to show how the flame spread after Mr. Cook had left St. Austell. Mr. Anderson writes: "We had one hundred and twenty converts in our villages last week. The Bible Christians had fifty. The Primitive Methodists sixteen. The United Methodist Free Church fifteen." The following week he writes: "Last week we had ninety conversions; the Bible Christians over a hundred; the Primitives sixteen." In a subsequent letter he states, as we have remarked before, that "not less than a thousand persons amongst the various sections of Methodism have been converted since your mission here; and the work still goes on."

At St. Ives the way of the Lord had been well prepared, and the work of reaping began as soon as the mission commenced. When the Evangelist went to the seat of war to reconnoitre, he found that the vestries which had been set apart as inquiry-rooms were unsuitable, and he asked the Rev. J. E. Hargreaves if he could not provide better accommodation. Mr. Hargreaves is well known to be a man of resource, and he suggested that the difficulty might be surmounted by knocking a hole through the wall at the right hand side of the pulpit, and thus making a way into convenient rooms not otherwise accessible. With characteristic boldness he arranged to have the alteration made forthwith, and the result was that next morning the trustees found that their property had been altered, not only without the consent of the Connexional Chapel Committee, but also without their own consent. But as the offence which David committed when he ate the shewbread, "which was not lawful for him to eat," was condoned because God desires "mercy and not sacrifice," so the offence of the superintendent minister, who was aided and abetted by the Evangelist, was likewise condoned for pretty much the same reason.

This action, in extemporising a doorway for the converts before the mission began, was not unlike the action of the priests when they placed their feet in the waters of Jordan; and as the faith of the priests was justified by the receding of the river, so the faith of the superintendent and the Evangelist was justified by the use which the converts made of the aperture created for their convenience. "Make this valley full of ditches" was the Lord's command in a time of great drought; for before the water was sent, channels were to be prepared for its reception. A great revival would surprise some of us, and therefore it does not come; whereas, if we made ready for an outpouring of the Spirit of God, we should not be put to shame.

At the first Sunday-night service at St. Ives a man called out audibly for mercy, and thus began a real work of grace. On the same day a gentleman who attended the mission took strong objection to Mr. Cook's teaching about the final penalties of sin. He was a man of intelligence, and, like many others, he had become fascinated with the doctrine of the "Larger Hope," and led to cherish expectations about the ultimate condition of those who persist in sin for which the Bible gives no ground. "Mr. Cook's God is not mine, nor is his doctrine mine," said the objector. Mr. Cook replied, "God will vindicate the truth." This God did in a most remarkable manner. Three or four days after, Mr. Cook received a message from the wife of the gentleman, to the effect that her husband was ill, and desired the favour of a visit from the Evangelist. Of course Mr. Cook went to see him. He found him very ill, suffering from pneumonia, and, as often happens with those who fear the Lord and know His secrets, Mr. Cook was convinced that the sickness was unto death. The dying man asked Mr. Cook to pray with him, but Mr. Cook suggested that this was useless, unless he was willing to "forsake his way." "Will you serve God for the rest of your life," said the Evangelist, "in case you are spared?" "Oh, yes," he replied, "my mind is fully made up; but call the family into the room, and I will commit myself to a new life in their presence."

This was done, and the penitent man repeated to his loved ones what he had said to the Evangelist. The family then retired, and the Evangelist betook himself to prayer, with the result that, before the interview ended, the sick man was enabled to say, "It is all right, Mr. Cook; God has been merciful to me." He then fell back exhausted, and soon afterwards expired; but he left behind him a clear testimony that the Lord Jesus had received his "soul at last."

It is not intended to censure this convert when it is said that thus God vindicated His Word, as though there were some connection between his former opinions and his death. All that is meant is, that God gave him to see that "Mr. Cook's God" is "merciful and gracious, longsuffering, and abundant in goodness and truth; keeping mercy for thousands; forgiving iniquity, transgression, and sin; *and that will by no means clear the guilty.*" This sheaf also will the Evangelist bring with him when he comes again rejoicing.

Night after night the work went on. Strong men bowed before the Lord; and some prominent townspeople were amongst the saved. On the second Sunday evening of the mission, a man left the service before it was closed, and arrived home much earlier than his praying wife expected him. She did not conceal her disappointment as she said, "I am sorry you are come home; I hoped you would be converted to-night." "I have come home *to be* converted," said the husband; "and I want you to pray with me." She did so, and the man was saved in his own house. He then hastened to the chapel to report what God had done for his soul. He afterwards told the Evangelist that it was not a sermon that brought him to decision, but reflection upon a remark made by his child two years before. The boy said to his mother, "When I am a man, I shan't say my prayers; father doesn't pray, and I shan't."

The mayor of the town, himself a member of the New Connexion body, bore testimony to the fact that a large number of intelligent men and women were brought to God by this mission; and musical readers will like to know that the organist and nearly every member of the choir, not excepting the organ-blower, —who must, at least by courtesy, be considered as belonging to the number,—were amongst the fruits of this mission. Several fishermen were also brought to God. One of these manifested his joy in a manner peculiar to himself. When he found salvation, he exclaimed, times without number, " Oh, beautiful Jesus! Oh, wonderful Jesus!" finishing up by calling out, " Three cheers for Jesus!" To some who do not know the human heart, this may seem irreverent. But others will not judge it to be so. Let every man declare *in his own tongue* the wonderful works of God! The Rev. Dr. Moulton visited St. Ives some little time after the mission, and during his year of office as President of the Conference. He saw some of the effects of the gracious work of which we have written, and in the Nottingham Conference he bore generous testimony to what he had witnessed.

From the fact that, fifteen months after the Camborne mission, seven hundred of the converts of that mission were meeting in the Society-classes, it will be seen by the candid reader that, although some of the phenomena connected with Cornish revivals are sufficiently perplexing, the results are, as Mr. W Bickford-Smith affirmed, seen in the permanent extension of the work of God. " Should it be according to *thy* mind?" we might ask some persons with reason, who, like Naaman, have their preconceived notions of the precise way in which the Spirit of God should work. " What was I, that I could withstand God?" asked

Peter, when he was put on his defence for a daring ecclesiastical innovation which he had introduced, and which he had been led to adopt by special intimation from heaven. "For it is written, I will destroy the wisdom of the wise, and will bring to nothing the understanding of the prudent." "Because the foolishness of God is wiser than men, and the weakness of God is stronger than men."

We have much reason to be proud of Cornish Methodism. The larger towns in Cornwall—Redruth, Falmouth, Truro, Penzance, and Camborne—all have noble chapels that may well excite the envy of other parts of the Connexion; while the county is dotted over with smaller Wesleyan chapels, which serve as the religious homes of the plain people who live in the more rural parts of that delightful tract of country. What is more: these Wesleyan-Methodist chapels are filled with devout, loyal, earnest Methodists, who are the strength of the land, and an honour to the Church of Christ.

Cornwall has enriched our ministry again and again with noble men, who have served Methodism loyally and to great advantage,—men who have been amongst our very best preachers. If, therefore, there is any part of England where we ought to retain our hold,—if there is any one county amongst all the English counties which may be said to be peculiarly ours, because we have won it by dint of hard evangelistic labour, abundantly blessed by God,—surely that county is Cornwall; and, consequently, if any Church—be that Church what it may—seeks to paralyse Methodism in Cornwall, not only will "forty thousand" Cornish Methodists "know the reason why," but the whole

Connexion will rally round this beloved plot, and protect it from the ecclesiastical invader.

The Cornish Circuits were perhaps never better manned as a whole than they are at the present time, and to this circumstance must be attributed much of the present prosperity of Methodism in that district. Far be it from the present writer to insinuate that there are *any* weak brethren in the Wesleyan ministry. No doubt "he that is feeble" is fully persuaded in his own mind that he is quite competent to discharge the duties of the Bishop of Truro, and it would be impertinent if the writer were to dissent from that view. But the writer trusts he will give no offence when he ventures to say, that although the whole of the Wesleyan ministry may be strong and well equipped, still, since there are some members of that body who are considered by their brethren to be more vigorous and better furnished than others, they are the men whom the past services and the present needs of Cornish Methodism demand should be sent to fill the pulpits of Cornwall.

CHAPTER XI.

FRAGMENTS THAT REMAIN.

IT is not intended to give anything like an exhaustive account in this small book of the whole of Mr. Cook's early ministry; but merely to sketch as much of that ministry as may be necessary in order to show that the Lord our God Himself has raised up unto us an Evangelist like unto the evangelists of early Methodism, and that God has in these modern days crowned the preaching of His Word with a blessing like that with which He crowned the preaching of our fathers.

We cannot live upon the past. The gracious services of the Centenary of Wesley's death were followed by the Œcumenical Conference in Washington; and these proceedings in England and the United States have filled us almost to satiety with admiration of the men who have made Methodism what it is. But this enlarging upon our noble ancestry has made us produce, not our discharge, but our debt; and we are bound to remember that we are debtors both to the men of the closing years of the nineteenth century and to those of the twentieth century. We know what the Methodism of the past was: what will the

Methodism of the future be? In the hope that this book may, by the Divine blessing, do something to make the Methodism of the future not unworthy of the Methodism of the past, it is, not without some misgiving, sent into the world.

The writer has not been able to use much more than half of the material that has been ready to his hand, partly on account of the exigencies of space, and partly on account of the delicate nature of some of that material. Few ties are more sacred than that which binds the convert to the evangelist who, in Christ Jesus, has begotten him through the gospel. The tie of parent and child, and of husband and wife, is in some respects not more sacred. The writer has endeavoured to exercise his discretion most carefully, in order that he may not be the means of publishing on the housetop that which was done or told in secret. How far he has succeeded in exercising proper discretion those chiefly concerned will have to determine. If they should think that he has been indiscreet, he begs them to exonerate Mr. Cook, who has placed his correspondence in his friend's hands, and relied on his judgment entirely as to the use that should be made of it. Mr. Cook must therefore be acquitted of all blame, and any censure that should be deserved must be visited upon the writer, and not upon the Evangelist. And, lest the writer should be too severely condemned by any sensitive reader, he craves leave to say, that what he has written he has written after due consideration, and with only one desire, namely, to increase the usefulness of the book, and thus to promote the glory of Him whose we are, and whom reader and writer alike serve.

> "O that I might now decrease!
> O that all I am might cease!
> Let me into nothing fall,
> Let my Lord be all in all!"

What minister is there who would not count it a great honour if it were to please God to use him as the instrument in His hands for quickening the ministers of the Churches? Higher honour than this, perhaps, no man can have, and this great privilege it has pleased God to confer on Mr. Cook, notwithstanding his youth and disadvantages. Letters might be printed from well-known ministers who have laboured with Mr. Cook in the gospel, and who write to express their gratitude, not only to the Giver of all good, but to His servant also by whose ministry God has called them nearer to Himself, and made them more "meet for the Master's use," and better "prepared unto every good work."

It is sometimes said that ministers are severe critics of their own order; and the writer himself being of that order, as well as the son of a minister, is not prepared to say that the statement is wholly without foundation. He has heard ministers criticise each other; he himself has had the temerity to undertake this function, although having no more authority to do it than any of his brethren. Nevertheless, he is prepared to affirm that, on the whole, Methodist preachers treat each other with a generousness that leaves nothing to be desired, and that often fills some of them with a deep sense of personal unworthiness. The warmest words of encouragement that the writer has ever had addressed to him, the words that have helped him most to combat constitutional timidity, and not to bury in the earth through fear his one talent, but to trade with it as much as may be, these words have been spoken to him by his own brethren at whose feet he would gladly have sat had Providence permitted him to do so.

It is not, therefore, surprising that amongst those who have taken the pains to express their indebtedness to Mr. Cook, are many ministers who have been led by him to see more fully what is the hope of their own calling in Christ Jesus. These letters shall not be published; the names of the writers shall not be disclosed; but the hope may be expressed that the blessings which they have received, and to which their letters bear testimony, may continue with them to the end of life, and make them, like Joseph, fruitful boughs, whose branches shall run over the wall! May their bow abide in strength, and the arms of their hands be made strong by the hands of the mighty God of Jacob!

A revived ministry will be followed by a revived Church; and a revived Church will be followed by a converted world. No harm will be done by publishing the following letter, written in a beautiful though trembling hand by one who was at the time of writing on the borderland:—" An aged Friend who has greatly enjoyed a few of thy meetings, being drawn into sympathy with thee, and prayer for rich blessing upon thyself and thy work, gives thee a copy of the late Rowland Hill's beautifully condensed invitation to sinners. She heard his earnest pleadings, and rejoices *now* to hear the same passing through the lips of a young David, anointed by the Divine Master to contend with the Goliath of evil! May His richest blessings rest upon thee!"

There is but one religion. The religion of the Friend and of the Methodist are the same, so far as it *is* religion at all.

> "Love, like death, hath all destroyed;
> Rendered all distinctions void:
> Names, and sects, and parties fall;
> Thou, O Christ, art all in all."

A lady, the mistress of a girls' school, writes to say that in her establishment many have been saved. She says: "There are twenty who profess to love the Saviour; in many, if not in all, there is a marked change. Your counsel has been a great blessing to my own heart. I do feel I can surrender all to God. There are still ten unsaved in my home; will you pray for them?"

Of Maidstone, as of many other places to which God has sent His servant, nothing has yet been written. A few words must suffice. A correspondent writes: "The memory of your visit to Maidstone will be very precious for many years to come. At Union Street alone we have gathered into the Society-classes more than seventy fresh adult members, and at Tonbridge Road more than fifty, whilst most of the country places have been strengthened. One place has received ten converts, another six, and so on. It is quite within the mark to say that there are at least one hundred and fifty new members on trial, as the direct result of the mission. Most of the Church people have, as we anticipated, returned to their own places of worship, although there are a few exceptions, where they have thrown in their lot with us."

The Rev. W. J. Cooke writes more than one glowing account of work in Leek, where some hundreds of converts were gathered in. Some months after the mission he reports two hundred and ninety-five members on trial in his Circuit, with thirty-two more who are reckoned as new members, and he adds that but few had been lost during the quarter. A Circuit minister writes of his Circuit, which had perhaps better not be named: " You have no idea how much heart this mission has put in me. I was on the edge of despair concerning the work here, but now I see signs of great things in both town and country. There will much good arise from this mission yet. We are having conversions in several of the villages, and I believe now that the Circuit will go up." Another correspondent, whose identity it will perhaps be wise to conceal,—after giving a glowing description of the results of a mission which Mr. Cook held in his Circuit, and sending an analysis of the converts, showing to how many various Churches they belonged, and telling of large prayer-meetings and many conversions attending the ordinary services,—remarks: " We need your prayers continually In some quarters there is still a tendency to discount the work of the mission, and after such glorious results this underrating of God's work is to me most depressing and discouraging. I don't talk about this, except to my wife, but I find that others are feeling as I do. However, in God is my trust. He will help us." The reader will supply his own comment. Let not any one suppose that the inquirers are all easily saved. We have already seen that such is not the case, and that the violent take the kingdom of heaven by force. Here is another proof of this. A correspondent writes to express thanks to God, and to the Evangelist, for blessing received during a mission, and he states that the first sermon she heard Mr. Cook preach made her unhappy, the next convinced her of sin, and on the morning of the third day of the mission she found peace with God at home, after having spent nearly all the night in private prayer.

Here are six young women in Bradford, "all intimate friends," who send a sort of round-robin in which they confess the blessing they have received during a mission held by the Evangelist in their town. From Holmfirth come tidings both pleasing and sad. A girl who was converted at one of Mr. Cook's services in that town, was caught in the shaft of the mill by her hair, and drawn up and instantly killed. Thus was another brand which had been plucked out of the burning preserved for ever from falling again into the burning.

A young lady writes from London to say that the mission she attended had stimulated her to begin to work for Christ. This she had done, and now she writes with overflowing joy of her first success. A man invited by her to chapel had accepted the invitation, and found salvation; and in the love-feast he had testified to the fact, and acknowledged her instrumentality. She is filled with thankfulness at the knowledge that her crown will not be without a star.

A minister sends word of a genuine conversion, proved by this circumstance, that the young lady in question had at the time of the mission engaged to go to two balls, one being the Licensed Victuallers', and the other the Jewish ball, and had prepared dresses for the occasion. But as soon as she was saved, "the expulsive power of a new affection" cast out that love of the world which is incompatible with the love of God, and balls and ball-dresses were put away for better delights.

By this means, no doubt, will worldly amusements be cast out of the Church. Mere denunciation will not prevent our unconverted young people from indulging in them, but a sound conversion to God will do this.

A member of Society writes to describe the great blessing which he has received at a holiness-meeting, and makes the strange admission that although he has been a member of the Methodist Society for eight years he had never heard of the doctrine until Mr. Cook instructed him in it.

The lamented Rev. Ishmael Jones, himself a bright example of the truth of perfect love, once told the writer that he attended a holiness convention on one occasion, when a speaker expatiated on the land of Canaan as a type, not of heaven, but of that rest of faith and love which remains *here* for the people of God, and into which they that believe have *now* entered. A clergyman of the Church of England was present at that service, and at the close of it he expressed to Mr. Jones how much he had been impressed with the teaching just described, which, indeed, he said had come to him with all the force of a revelation, he never having heard that view enunciated before. The Wesleyan minister then told him that the teaching to which he had that day listened with so much surprise and delight was no new truth to Methodists, since it had been embodied in Methodist hymnology for well-nigh a hundred and fifty years. In proof of this statement, Mr. Jones then quoted to the clergyman our hymns commencing, "O glorious hope of perfect love," and "Lord, I believe a rest remains." When the quotations were finished, the clergyman responded, "How beautiful! And do all your ministers and people enjoy this blessing?"

The answer of the Wesleyan minister, who is now with God, need not be given; but all will know what he fain *would* have said in reply to that natural, but to us humbling, question.

Must the great and glorious truth of perfect love be left by the Methodists to be taught by the Salvation Army, who, of course, received it from us? God forbid we should leave it to them! This is the more to be deprecated, because there is some reason to fear that the leaders of that movement are now giving less attention to the great *depositum* committed by God to our care, than they did in the earlier years of the history of their wonderful organisation. Whether it is that they are otherwise engaged, or whether some other explanation must be given, the fact remains that, like the denomination which is their prototype, the Salvation Army have gradually given less and less attention, so far as an outsider can judge, to this momentous truth. What are we doing, that we allow persons to remain for years within our communion without pressing upon them the absolute duty of claiming from God, by simple faith in Christ Jesus, the instantaneous blessing of perfect love? Entire sanctification is not believed by us to be an optional blessing. We have learned, if only from the sixth chapter of the Epistle to the Romans, that it was inconceivable to the apostles that any one who was in Christ, and who consequently was "dead to sin," should "live any longer therein;" and what we have learned we are bound to teach, and to keep "back nothing that [will be] profitable" unto "the flock over the which the Holy Ghost hath made [us] overseers, to feed the Church of God, which He hath purchased with His own blood." Had the experience of this member of eight years' standing been a solitary experience, not so much need have been said about it; but as it is to be feared that he represents many others, it has seemed right to the author to make some considerable use of his declaration.

Scholars will be interested in a letter written from St. John's College, Cambridge, of which, as it bears on the subject just referred to, an extract shall be given. The writer says: "Your visit has done us all good, especially the undergraduates, a good many of whom are earnestly seeking the blessing of the 'Higher Life.' I am going to have some of them in my rooms next week, that we may have a talk and a small prayer-meeting about it. May I ask your prayers for us? Will you kindly tell me the name of the American publishers of that book, Dr. Steele's *Milestone Papers?* A Cambridge bookseller is going to send over to the States for a copy of it, and wants the publisher's address. If you will send it, you will make half-a-dozen of us feel indebted to you."

Here the reader sees half-a-dozen Cambridge men earnestly seeking the blessing of entire sanctification, for which God be praised; and he also sees them laboriously endeavouring to get from America a book which their religious teacher had recommended to them. Mr. Cook often recommends other books on this subject, such as Hunt's *Letters*, Fletcher's *Last Check*, Wood's

Perfect Love, and Steele's *Love Enthroned* (all of which may be obtained from the Wesleyan Book Room); but we wish to embrace this opportunity of saying that there is great room in this country for a really able, scholarlike, scriptural, and popular work on holiness as it was understood and taught by the founders of Methodism. The sections in Dr. Pope's great compendium on theology that refer to this theme are, of course, invaluable, as is also his *Prayers of St. Paul*, which the late B. A. Gregory found more serviceable to him than any other book that deals with the doctrine. But Dr. Pope's works are written for students, properly so called, and his teaching, like the courage and skill of Mr. Valiant-for-Truth, is for "him that can get it."

The Rev. Dr. Beet's treatise on Holiness is useful, and meets a real want, as is proved by the fact that there is a constant demand for it year by year. But that publication also is adapted chiefly to readers of studious habits, who are accustomed to rather close thinking. Moreover, Dr. Beet does not dwell sufficiently on the *Methodist* aspect of the doctrine, and his pamphlet leaves much to be desired, when it is wanted, for such readers as attend holiness-meetings, not excepting these Cambridge scholars. There are, of course, many good devotional books which deal more or less thoroughly with the doctrine, but there is not in circulation precisely the kind of book which is needed, and which, if once it was written by a competent hand, who must be a ripe scholar as well as a profound theologian, and fully in sympathy with the Wesleyan Hymn-book presentation of the truth, would sell by the thousand. The Book Committee would render the Connexion a service if they could induce such a writer to take this work in hand; and were they to look in the neighbourhood of Handsworth, it is certain they would find the desiderated writer.

Mr. Cook has been able to reach large numbers of people by his pen as well as his voice. He has not yet published anything of much size, but his penny booklets have had an immense sale. A hundred thousand copies of his *First Steps in the Way of Life* have been sold, and the demand still continues. Forty thousand copies of his first publication on *Scriptural Perfection* have been circulated, and ten thousand copies of his *Entire Cleansing* were sold within a short time of its being issued from the press, and another edition has been printed. Other booklets have also been published by him, and have met with a warm reception.

The value of this means of imparting instruction is very great. There is no doubt a charm about the voice which is lacking in what appears in cold type; but against this drawback must be set off the advantage which printed matter has over oral, in that it may be read and re-read in the quiet of one's own room when one is fully awake, and not distracted by other allurements. It should also be said that Mr. Cook has assisted in establishing an organisation which is known as the "Out-and-Out Band," and which, under the joint control of the Revs. P Thompson, J G. Mantle, and himself, is conducted with a view to deepen the spiritual life of the members, and to secure their influence for the furtherance of the gospel. The band now numbers fourteen thousand members, of whom a large proportion are the fruits of Mr. Cook's ministry The association is kept together by a monthly publication, thirty-five thousand copies of which were printed for the November issue, 1891, that number being specially adapted for the week of prayer, which was observed by the Connexion during that month. No controversial matter is ever introduced into that serial, the object of which is purely devotional, and therefore the larger the circulation it enjoys, the more reason we all shall have to rejoice.

The members of the Out-and-Out Band are encouraged to take an interest in aggressive work, as well as to engage in such service themselves. An Out-and-Out Band Gospel Mission Car Association has been formed, the object of which is to build and place on the road gospel cars, each of which costs £150, and is under the care of two earnest Christian men, who act as colporteurs and evangelists, visiting chiefly small towns and villages. Each car is stocked with religious literature, and the agents in charge sell the books from house to house during the day-time, and hold services in the chapels in the evening. Three cars are now employed under the direction of the Home Mission Sub-Committees of the Newcastle, Leeds, and Lincoln districts; and it is expected that a fourth car will soon be sent to Ireland, and that ere long ten or twelve cars may be at work in various parts of the Connexion. The initial cost is the only expense incurred, for once a car is opened and placed in good hands, it becomes self-supporting. It will thus be seen that these gospel cars are likely to become a valuable arm of the service. By circulating wholesome literature much good will be done. The colporteurs in charge of one of the cars lately sold twenty pounds' worth of books in a single week in a country town, and the sales are constantly increasing.

The services which the colporteurs hold in the village chapels and on the village greens will also do much to promote the evangelisation of rural England.

The work of the Out-and-Out Band is twice blessed. It blesses those to whom the agents are sent, and it blesses the members of the band who send them, and who are thus led to look beyond their own Circuits, and to take an intelligent and practical interest in the conversion of their fellow-creatures. Moreover, the organisation does a great deal to help the new converts to retain their steadfastness. In many ways it enables the Evangelist to keep in touch with his children, and to let them understand that *now he lives, if they stand fast in the Lord.* It should be added that it is the duty of the local secretaries of the Out-and-Out Band to watch over all the members of the organisation living in their district, and to report to the general secretaries any cases of defection of which they may become cognisant. Although, as we have seen, the Out-and-Out Band now numbers fourteen thousand members, the general secretaries have heard of scarcely more than fifty members who have fallen away. The conditions of membership are: A striving after personal experience of scriptural holiness; an earnest effort to bless some soul every day; committing to memory the motto words chosen, and the reading of the selected portions of Scripture; and daily prayer for all the members of the band, that they may be filled with the Holy Ghost. It is cause for thankfulness that so many thousands have bound themselves by these rules, and if the Lord our God should "add unto the people, how many soever they be, an hundredfold," it would be a signal blessing to our beloved Church.

CHAPTER XII.

RESULTS OF THE WORK.

DURING the course of an edifying conversation which took place in the First London District Committee at their September meeting in 1891, the Rev. Dr. Jenkins cautioned his brethren against undervaluing everything of the nature of success which cannot be represented as the net result of ministerial labour in the columns of a schedule. He declared that God knew nothing of such net results, and he pointed out to an audience in full sympathy with him, that a minister was not to measure the amount of his success *simply* by the number of penitents whom he persuaded to enter the inquiry-room. The present writer was in agreement with Dr. Jenkins on that occasion, only he takes leave to think that the danger against which Dr. Jenkins warned his brethren is not *the* danger to which they are most exposed. We are rather liable to suppose that we are successful, even though we persuade *none* of our hearers to "enter the inquiry-room."

The work of the evangelist, like that of the Circuit minister, cannot all be tabulated. Not that we wish to disparage statistics. Some member of the apostolic Church deemed it proper to count the number of converts on the day of Pentecost, and although the inspired historian does not vouch for strict accuracy, he does undertake to fix approximately the number of those who that day judged themselves worthy of everlasting life.

The account of that first revival in the history of Christianity is rendered all the more vivid and inspiring, by the exact information that is given when we are told, "and the same day there were added unto them about *three thousand* souls." Nor is this the only instance in which the New Testament sets us the example of counting the converts. In a later chapter we are told of "five thousand" who believed, and were added to the Church. When, therefore, we are reminded in this connection of the numbering of the people by David, we retort that the cases are not similar, and that it is a distinct advantage to know what numerical increase the Church of Christ is able to report. The world is to be converted to Jesus Christ, and therefore it is important that we should ascertain by the aid of figures how far aggressive work is prospering. It is not a matter of indifference to us whether there are ten converts at a given mission or ten hundred; and when the latter is the correct number, it is well to let all the world know. At the time of writing Mr. Cook has just held a mission in a Circuit chapel, where he was told that for seven years no conversion had been known to take place. The sterility of that Church has been notorious, and now that God has given it a season of comparative plenty, why should not that be known as widely as the seven years of leanness?

Nevertheless it is important to remember that only

"the day will declare" all the good that any servant of Christ has done. "Every man shall receive his own reward according to his own labour."

All evangelists have been told that their work was ephemeral. John Wesley was told this, and yet a hundred years after his death there are five-and-twenty millions of Methodists in the world, and the probability is that Methodism will continue until the sign of the Son of man appears in heaven. The same objection was raised against the work of Dr. and Mrs. Palmer and of Mr. Moody, and, of course, it has been raised against the work of Mr. Cook.

Some years ago, the Rev. Joseph Cook, of Boston, addressing an audience of three thousand people, asked those who were converted to stand up. Two thousand five hundred did so. He then asked those who had been brought to God in revival services to remain standing and the others to resume their seats. Those who continued to stand were counted, and the number was found to be "about" fifteen hundred. The writer himself once made a similar experiment at a service in Manchester, and the result was such as makes the above story quite credible to him. Somewhere about the year 1850 a series of special services was held in a small village of four hundred inhabitants. At one of the services six penitents "came out," and forty years afterwards five of the six were walking in the fear of the Lord and in the comfort of the Holy Ghost. The Rev. Featherstone Kellett was one, the Rev. T. Nattrass, now with God, was another, Mr. Joshua Dawson and his wife were two more, and the steward of a Circuit in the north of England was the fifth.

Mr. E. B. Dingley, of Sherborne, took the trouble to keep a register of the persons added to the Sherborne Society for about thirty years, with the circumstances and date of their conversion. It was found on examination that "about"—for I wish to imitate St. Luke's caution—eighty per cent. of all the additions to that Society during that period were the fruit of mission services.

At the same time, it must be frankly admitted that mission services have their disappointments. A short time before his death, Dr. Osborn, in a private conversation with the writer, took occasion to descant on the number of backsliders over whom Methodism has to mourn, and he advised the writer to ascertain from the Minutes of Conference the number of members whom Methodism has lost during the twenty-one years of the writer's ministry.

The probability is that if such a calculation were made with anything approaching to accuracy, it would be found that the number of members who have "ceased to meet" during that period would be equal to the entire membership of the Connexion at the present time.

If such returns had been made in the lifetime of Dr. Osborn, and the writer's computation had been correct, no one would have been less surprised than that astute minister, seeing that it was a conviction of his that Methodism is like a great draw-net, which gathers fish "of every kind," as, indeed, the writer has heard him say. Cornish readers especially will appreciate this reference to the parable of the draw-net.

On the coast of Cornwall, as we ourselves have found, the "sean" or "draw-net" is a familiar sight

"Sometimes the 'sean' will be half a mile long. Leaded below, that it may sweep the bottom of the sea, and supported with corks above, it is carried out so as to enclose a large space of sea; the ends are then brought together, and the "sean," with all its contents, is drawn up upon the shore."

So is the kingdom of heaven, according to the teaching of its Divine Founder. So it is always, but especially when it is set forth in mission services.

Many who profess conversion on such occasions doubtless have not experienced any real change of heart. The parable of the Sower is a sort of history of the preached Word. Some converts are like the rocky ground, others are like the thorny ground; and hence "fruit unto perfection" is more rare than some enthusiastic mission preachers are willing to believe. Nevertheless, *some* "fruit unto life eternal" is gathered by the God-sent reaper.

One explanation of the comparative smallness of the numerical increase which mission services sometimes produce, is found in the incredulity of leaders who have no confidence in the stability of converts, and from the first act on the assumption that they will *not* stand. Some of Mr. Cook's converts' names have been placed by leaders on loose sheets of paper, and never inscribed in the class-books, because the leaders, strange to say, had foreknowledge of their defection, and wished to prepare for what they regarded as inevitable. If new-born children were treated as new-born souls are sometimes treated, the rate of infant mortality, now appallingly high, would be perceptibly increased. When the late Rev. W O. Simpson was an infant he was puny and unpromising, and his parents, afraid that they would not be able to rear him, called in the Rev. R. Treffry, and asked him to baptize the child in private. But William O. Simpson lived for fifty years. He would not have done so, however, if his mother had exposed him and nourished him ill. Good nursing and good nourishment have prolonged the lives of many feeble infants.

And good Christian nursing and good Christian teaching will, by the Divine blessing, succeed in prolonging the lives of many new-born souls. St. Paul was gentle among his converts, "even as a nurse cherisheth her children:" he "exhorted, and comforted, and charged *every one of them*, as a father doth his children;" for were they not his "glory" and his "joy"? If pastors and sub-pastors, as our class-leaders have been justly called, had a greater measure of this Pauline spirit, would not more of our converts stand? "Of them which Thou hast given Me, I have lost none, but the son of perdition, that the scripture might be fulfilled." So said our Lord Jesus, that Great Shepherd of the sheep. Converts are not "given" to under-shepherds in the same sense as souls are "given" to Christ. But they are committed to the *care* of under-shepherds, and the more care we take of them the more likely are we to "receive a crown of life" when "the Chief Shepherd shall appear."

The kind of enlargement that our leaders' meetings most need is the enlargement of their spiritual functions. The leaders as sub-pastors are called to watch over the souls of the members of Society, that, with the pastors, they may "present every man perfect in Christ Jesus." Would it not be well to hold leaders' meetings for distinctively spiritual purposes more frequently? If leaders would attend the leaders' meeting, if they would bring their class-books with them, if they would be careful to mark their class-books as they are directed to do in the instructions furnished to them within the covers of those books, and if more time at the leaders' meeting was devoted to taking the oversight of the flock, and labouring fervently in prayer for the Church, as Epaphras did for the Church of Colosse, that the members might stand perfect and complete in all the will of God,—if these things were better done, should we not have less cause for mourning over the unfaithfulness of our converts?

Another explanation of the smallness of the net result of mission services is found in this circumstance, —the names of many old members are dropped by their leaders as soon as the leaders obtain new ones to take their places. Leaders and pastors have a natural dread of decreases; and therefore dead branches are not always lopped off as soon as they die, but are often permitted to hang on the tree for a time, until they can be severed from the tree without attracting much notice. As soon as a fruitful season comes, this opportunity arrives, and then the pruning-knife is used vigorously. The result is, that although the Society is thus made more sound and healthy, the membership shows little or no increase, and the uninitiated ask with amazement, "What has become of the converts?" In some Circuits the converts are kept "on trial" for an unconscionable time, and are used as the reserves are used in the military world. That is, they are called upon to supply vacancies, and used skilfully, in order that the Circuits in question should not be reduced to the necessity of reporting decreases. In one case the Evangelist happened to know that a certain Circuit in which he had held a mission had received an accession of two hundred members, and yet he noticed that the Circuit did not report any increase at the March quarterly meeting. Thereupon he wrote and made inquiries, and he was told in reply that he might be quite comfortable about the fruits of the mission; he was to do himself no harm, they were all there; but they had not been reported "because the Circuit could not undertake any additional financial responsibility."

If the appeal is unto figures, unto figures we must go, but the whole case must be disclosed, and not merely a part of it. When the work of God is discredited owing to our peculiarities in the method of returning members, it is time that the truth should be told at all costs.

It must also never be forgotten that the fruits of our missions are distributed amongst all the Churches. This has been seen again and again in our review of Mr. Cook's work, but it needs to be often re-stated, that we may be preserved from discouragement. The late James Chalmers was wont to say that one of the brightest crowns of Methodism was that which she wears as the result of the service she has rendered to other Churches. A striking proof of this was seen on one occasion in the house of the late Rev. Dr. Jobson. That deceased minister once entertained at dinner a number of the most prominent Nonconformist ministers in London, and, after the meal was over, he characteristically suggested that a love-feast should be held, and proceeded at once to ask his reverend guests what were the means by which they were brought to God. The Rev. Dr. Allon, the venerable minister of Union Chapel, Islington, said that he was convinced of sin whilst he was a member of the Wesleyan congregation in Beverley, where he was brought to decision, and became a Sunday school teacher and member of Society. The late Dr. Raleigh declared that he learnt the way of faith in the Brunswick Wesleyan Chapel, Liverpool. The Rev. Dr. Stoughton testified that he found comfort and help in St. Peter's Wesleyan Chapel, Norwich, where he was for a while a member of Society, meeting in class with the grandfather of the Rev. F. L. Wiseman, B.A., of the Birmingham mission. Dr. Binney and Dr. Fraser both expressed their great indebtedness to Methodism—the former to a Methodist workman, and the latter to a Methodist lady. It thus unexpectedly transpired that all the five Nonconformist ministers present were the direct or indirect fruit of Methodist preaching and Methodist influence.

When the question is asked, " Where are the converts ? " it will often be correct to say, " Many of them are in the various Churches that lie outside our own communion, where they are serving under the ' One Shepherd,' who some day will have but ' one fold.' "

The following facts illustrative of the permanent results that attend the ministry of our Evangelist, will be welcomed by the sympathetic reader. A few years ago, Mr. Cook selected half-a-dozen places in which he had held missions, and took pains to ascertain what proportion of fruit the Wesleyan-Methodist

Church had permanently retained. He wrote to the ministers of the respective Circuits, than whom no better witnesses could be found, and asked them to make careful and exact records of the persons then meeting in the Society-classes who had been converted at the various missions. In the case of each Circuit more than a year had elapsed since the mission was held, and in the six Circuits the ministers reported that there were one thousand members attending the class-meetings, and giving their pastors continued cause for thankfulness and hope. In another Circuit, where the superintendent minister was dubious about the results of one of Mr. Cook's missions, a class-leader resolved to keep a correct list of the additions made to the Society at the time of the mission, and to watch their history for twelve months, and then report to the leaders' meeting. This was done, the result being that out of one hundred and fifty persons who joined Society at the close of the mission, one hundred and twenty-three were meeting in class after the interval of a year, which must certainly be considered as a not unsatisfactory result.

The Rev. Dr. Bowden confirms the testimony to which these statements point. He says: "In the Bristol district I was careful to notice the history of the Circuits, and I found that some Circuits often had mission services, and others seldom or never had them. The result was that the former Circuits prospered, while the others either remained stationary or decreased in members."

But enough has been written to convince all who are willing to be convinced, that whilst for the permanent extension of the work of God and the conversion of the world to the Lord Jesus Christ, we must mainly rely on the ordinary services of the Church, conducted by the ordained pastors of the Churches, assisted, of course, by voluntary and paid lay workers; the help of evangelists like Mr. Cook must be accepted gratefully, and cordially appreciated, and special missions must be organised more or less frequently in order that inroads upon the vice and irreligion of the country may be made to purpose, and the Church may be prevented from settling on its lees.

The writer has now finished his task. He has presented such a sketch of the early ministry of Mr. Cook as he has been able to do, and has made those observations which in his judgment the narrative is calculated to suggest to all Christians, and especially to members of his own Church. But before he lays down his pen and bids the reader a respectful adieu, he would fain add a few more sentences, in the hope that it may please God to use them to advance the cause which both evangelist and reader and writer have at heart.

However optimistic we may be, it is impossible to be entirely satisfied with the progress Methodism has made during recent years. When we consider our increased facilities for carrying on evangelistic work,—the press, the railway, the ability of the people to read, the open streets in which we may always secure a congregation, the number of our chapels, the wealth of our people, the learning of our ministers, the devotion of many of our people,—we are bound to admit that our chapels ought to be crowded, as well as our mission halls, and that our membership should go up by leaps and bounds.

It is well known that the *Times* has always been lacking in sympathy with the Salvation Army, and has not seldom written of General Booth and his work in an unfriendly, not to say positively antagonistic spirit. But some half-dozen years ago there appeared in the leading journal an article on the Salvation Army which seemed to me to be wise and instructive in a singular degree. The writer said: "Undoubtedly the Salvation Army has something in its spirit which other religious bodies need not disdain to copy. All old-established societies tend after a while to close their doors, and to turn their camps into citadels. The strength of the Salvation Army is that it is constantly in light marching order.
Its life is a life of forage and invasions. With all its defects, it will not have been without use, if, before the movement declines and dies out, it has reminded orderly communities of a distant past in which, at the opening of their career, they conducted themselves with the same vivacity." Our own "orderly community" did, indeed, "at the opening of its career" conduct itself with great vivacity, and what is sorely needed is that we should return in spirit and aim to the Methodism of our fathers. The times demand a great outburst of enthusiasm in the service of our Lord Jesus Christ. Many of us have made a gain of godliness. It has brought us comfort, social status, health, and in many instances affluence, and troops of friends. The time has come for us to make some extrordinary sacrifice for religion, and to *do* something which will tend to compensate the Saviour for His "dying love," if we may borrow the idea from one of our

own poets. "It is not the smallness of the work one can do for Christ that astonishes me," says a thoughtful writer, "it is the *greatness* of the work that one can do that fills me with amazement." The reader will judge how far this narrative confirms that observation, and the writer will only add that whatever success Thomas Cook has had in his early ministry, it must all be attributed to his absolute devotion to the Lord Jesus Christ, whose he is, and whom he serves.

www.ingramcontent.com/pod-product-compliance
Lightning Source LLC
Chambersburg PA
CBHW020756230426
43666CB00007B/715